Finding Your Way in Early Adulthood

Working Out What You Want & Choosing How to 'Be'

(A guide for navigating the early adult years)

Helen Middleton

First published by Busybird Publishing 2018
Copyright © 2018 Helen Middleton

ISBN
Print: 978-1-925830-02-6

Helen Middleton has asserted her right under the Copyright, Designs and Patents Act 1988 to be identified as the author of this work. The information in this book is based on the author's experiences and opinions. The publisher specifically disclaims responsibility for any adverse consequences, which may result from use of the information contained herein. Permission to use information has been sought by the author. Any breaches will be rectified in further editions of the book.

All rights reserved. No part of this publication may be reproduced, stored in or introduced into a retrieval system, or transmitted in any form, or by any means (electronic, mechanical, photocopying, recording or otherwise) without the prior written permission of the author. Any person who does any unauthorised act in relation to this publication may be liable to criminal prosecution and civil claims for damages. Enquiries should be made through the publisher.

Cover Illustration: Leonie De Salis
Cover Design: Kev Howlett, Busybird Publishing
Layout and typesetting: Busybird Publishing
Editor: Laura McCluskey

Busybird Publishing
2/118 Para Road
Montmorency, Victoria
Australia 3094
www.busybird.com.au

For Ariane and Leigh.

Contents

Acknowledgements   i

Preface   iii

1. Balancing work, study, relationships, and career aspirations   1
- 1.1. Summer holidays, and you still don't know what you want to do?   1
- 1.2. Understanding the post-school lull. Looking at options   3
- 1.3. Persevering with the option you choose   7
- 1.4. Adapting to your new life   10
- 1.5. If life feels like it is falling apart   15

2. Building employment prospects   19
- 2.1. Starting work   19
- 2.2. Having fun and building a good reputation at work   21
- 2.3. Dating in the workplace   24
- 2.4. Interpersonal dynamics in the workplace   25
- 2.5. Knowing your rights in the workplace   30

3. Nurturing yourself   31
- 3.1. Looking after your self-esteem and building resilience   31
- 3.2. Identifying the mental scripts that constrain you   34
- 3.3. Comparing yourself to others   36
- 3.4. Being bold – making yourself heard   38
- 3.5. Burnout   41
- 3.6. Overcoming stress, overthinking, and anxiety   42
- 3.7. Dealing with depression   53
- 3.8. Coping with loss   59

4. Getting serious about relationships — 65
- 4.1. What makes a relationship healthy? — 65
- 4.2. Contributing strength to your relationship — 70
- 4.3. How do you know when you have met the right partner? — 74
- 4.4. No matter what you do, it is just not working — 78

5. Secrets, and how to survive them — 91
- 5.1. Sexual abuse, and beating shame — 91
- 5.2. Trauma — 96
- 5.3. Thriving, instead of seeing yourself as a victim — 100

6. Emotional intelligence in the workplace — 103
- 6.1. Becoming a manager — 103
- 6.2. Working alongside other managers — 107
- 6.3. Dealing with difficult personalities — 109
- 6.4. Having hard conversations with those you supervise — 113
- 6.5. Work/life balance — 116
- 6.6. When those you supervise have special skills — 117
- 6.7. Working under higher management — 118

7. Creating family — 121
- 7.1. Sustaining relationships over the long-term — 121
- 7.2. Violence, anger, possession, and paranoia ... power and control — 132

8. The sensing child — 137
- 8.1. Learning from children — 137
- 8.2. The art of parenting — 140
- 8.3. The difference between tough love and abuse — 147
- 8.4. Children learning from parents and extended family — 150
- 8.5. Difficult times — 151

9. Understanding adolescents — 155
- 9.1. The developmental nature of adolescence — 155
- 9.2. Supporting adolescents — 158
- 9.3. Dealing with difficult behaviour and difficult times — 163

10. Step-parenting and blending families — 171
- 10.1. Relationships in times of transition — 171
- 10.2. Before you bring your new family unit together — 173
- 10.3. Becoming a solid family unit — 176
- 10.4. Step-parenting — 178
- 10.5. Attitudes that impede positive adjustment — 181
- 10.6. If disciplinary issues appear — 188
- 10.7. When the family unit settles and life starts to feel good — 191

11. Grief, transition and change — **195**
- 11.1. Life inevitably brings grief — 195
- 11.2. Emotional reactions and protracted grief — 199
- 11.3. On taking grief home — 200
- 11.4. Life is about persistence and living with uncertainty — 201

12. The wisdom of nurturing your soul — **205**
- 12.1. Believing in yourself — 205
- 12.2. Spirituality — 207
- 12.3. Going forward — 212

About the Author — **215**

Acknowledgements

I would like to acknowledge my many colleagues over the years. These include teachers, principals, deputies, guidance officers, gestalt and family therapists, psychotherapists, psychologists, youth workers, social workers, nurses, general practitioners, and other mental health professionals. I thank those who educated and trained me and I especially thank all the psychotherapy theorists and practitioners whose ideas I have tried to weave into practical applications in this book. I also appreciate those friends and colleagues who have helped in the process of editing. Thanks go to Leonie DeSalis for her cover illustration.

I would particularly like to acknowledge my husband, Michael, who has encouraged me to gain the qualifications and experience that led me to this publication.

Lastly, I would like to thank the many clients who honoured me by openly sharing their world with me. So often I have admired their fortitude, wisdom, and humour.

Preface

The content of this book has been put together in an attempt to give young people some background perspectives of the issues that often cause concern. The initial motivation for writing the book was to pass on to my own grandchildren some of the knowledge I have gained.

With each generation, life seems to become increasingly complex and my wish is to help young people develop a sound framework of knowledge and wisdom from which to navigate their own pathway.

I have drawn on my experiences working with young adults and have chosen to reflect psychological and psychotherapy principles applied in practice. I have avoided typical information that is easily sourced, and instead have addressed fundamental attitudes and perspectives that lead to wise choice-making. I have structured the book in sections that can be read in isolation according to interest. The chapters highlight common issues presented to me by young adults during counselling sessions.

After leaving school there are many aspects of life that present a struggle for young adults. They enter all the dimensions of adult life, many of which are full of complexity and require careful decision-making.

As young people engage in study, employment, and casual or volunteer work, they are also often confronted with issues in personal relationships. They grapple with forming their own identity, establishing their reputation and their way of being in the world. Beyond all this, they have to learn to balance life in a way that meets their immediate needs, as well as their long-term goals.

Young adults need to be well-informed. They need to work out what they want, and need to choose how they want to be in all aspects of their life. This book is designed to assist them.

1
Balancing work, study, relationships, and career aspirations

> *1.1. Summer holidays, and you still don't know what you want to do?*
>
> *1.2. Understanding the post-school lull. Looking at options*
>
> *1.3. Persevering with the option you choose*
>
> *1.4. Adapting to your new life*
>
> *1.5. If life feels like it is falling apart*

1.1. Summer holidays, and you still don't know what you want to do?

I have known many students who have been so focused on getting high results that they get to the end of Year 12 with no notion of their future career path. They have many options, but which one should they choose? They have covered career selection and goalsetting as part of career education at school, so they know the process. They find themselves in the middle of the summer holidays without an end goal. They have big decisions to make, but keep floating between possibilities. The choice of their future pathway depends on knowing what they want on many different levels.

If you are floundering and have no idea of what direction you wish to go, then take a little time to dream and to think about what interests you. What are the things you do that you enjoy, the things that bring you pleasure and happiness and a sense of achievement? Note the things that will build your capacity to learn and to earn. Think about your special talents. Do some online personality and career testing to become more familiar with who you are with all your strengths and weaknesses. Flexing your 'want' muscle takes a little training. Think about what you might like to be doing in five years' time.

On a daily basis do you want to work intensely with people, or on your own? Would you like to be outside or inside? Would you rather work with people or animals? Would you like to be in a caring role? Think of a range of careers that might interest you and narrow them down to an area of work or an industry that attracts you. For example, are you attracted to fields like engineering, health, arts, science, recreation, or education? Try not to rule out a job because of one thing you know you will dislike. If you can find a job where most of the elements appeal to you, you are doing well. There is usually some part of the work that is less attractive, or a little frustrating. Don't ignore your quirky talents. Take delight in your passions. Sometimes talent and experience come together in the most amazing ways. You might have various passions that seem unrelated at present, but later in life you might be surprised to find they come together to form an unusual combination that results in a niche role. The teacher who had a quirky mind for timetabling becomes a consultant. The kid nicknamed 'Bushranger' at school becomes the skilled negotiator. The gutsy young girl with learning difficulties sails around the world. Quirky skills and talents emerge naturally. They are not taught as part of a traditional curriculum, and yet, one day, they may prove to be your super strength.

It is okay to take a temporary job if the end goal is to save enough to give you a start in something you really want. Study, jobs, and careers can be hard if you don't have passion for an end goal. It can be a hard journey, especially when some of the tasks are boring or repetitive. Stick at it. If you are confident

1. Balancing work, study, relationships, and career aspirations

of the end goal then you will be well rewarded. Make sure that you are not caught up in some romantic notion of the career you have in mind. It might sound glamorous to be a celebrated doctor, pilot, or golf pro, but will you like the daily reality of those jobs? Make sure you have detailed knowledge of daily duties in any field after you have graduated.

For instance, it is no use having a fantasy about working with big machinery on a mine site if you are unable to tolerate living away from home, or working in hot, remote locations. Think through the realities of various careers. Follow your heart and your passions, without being naïve about the negatives. If the choice you make turns out not to suit you, you can always change direction.

1.2. Understanding the post-school lull. Looking at options

Many students don't realise that leaving school may be the most confusing time in their life. By the time the last day of school comes around, the last end of year party, and the last goodbye, everything changes. Suddenly there is no school on Monday! Friends go in all directions. They go on holiday, travel, make family Christmas visits, and move house. The busy schedule of study and the deadlines are gone, and the wait for Year 12 results is torturous. The usual feelings about routines fade, leaving you in an emotional void. Be mindful of this possibility and try to have things organised that you will look forward to.

Until now, most of your life will have been organised for you, and it is understandable that your first reaction during the post-school lull might be no schedules: 'I am not committing to anything'. That is the holiday feeling ... and how good is that for the first few weeks! Understand that while 'chill-out' time is important, it can lead to a 'lost' feeling after a few weeks. Plan a camping trip with mates, or some special activities that you love. You need to have places to go, people to see, and things to do. By February, you may be itching to start something new, to commence a new course of study, to settle into the freedom and excitement of tertiary life or employment, and to make new friends. When you have 'drained the cup' of holidays, ask yourself what you want from the forthcoming year.

It comes back to goals. Do you want a year of work while you save money for later travel? Do you want to throw yourself into full-time study or training? Do you want to do part-time study and part-time work, or specialise in a sporting pursuit? Does volunteer work interest you? What about special interest courses? Do you want to devote your time to music, or some other passion?

You can just let life happen, or you can shape your life to meet your 'wants'. Yes, it is time to ask some serious questions. I encourage you to choose boldly rather than merely follow what you think is expected of you. You might find this very hard, but it is worth challenging yourself.

Gap Year option
Think carefully if you are choosing a Gap Year plan. What opportunities are open to you? Will you volunteer overseas, work, travel, or undertake a learning program? Think about what you will get out of this Gap Year. Whatever you do needs to be worthwhile, because it would be unfortunate to waste one year of your life because your plan was not well developed. If you choose a Gap Year, plan it carefully and don't write off tertiary options in November just because you are tired of study. Keep your options open as long as you can. By February you just might be really keen to start a new course of study.

Choosing work over study options
If you choose to go to full-time work after leaving school, make sure you are on a learning path that gives you some training credentials. Make a plan and map out possible pathways as you gain more experience.

For instance, you may choose hospitality and have to take the first job that comes your way. The plan might be to build your confidence in café service, then look for opportunities

1. Balancing work, study, relationships, and career aspirations

to gain your Responsible Service of Alcohol (RSA) certificate and barista experience. After that the plan might be to look for ways to move into hotel service or to study front of house qualifications or to move into hotel management. Alternatively, your plan might be to one day own your own café so you then gradually work your way through a business management course. Dream your future pathway.

You might like cars but are unsure about being a motor mechanic. You might choose to start working in car detailing or start an apprenticeship as a mechanic, only to find that you have a passion for heavy-duty truck engines. Think broadly about where the skills you gradually acquire might take you. Successful futures do not all come from academic study. We live in a world that celebrates and uses practical intelligence and practical skills.

If you are feeling afraid to make a decision or have limited options for employment, have the courage to start somewhere. It is like venturing out in your car. If you just sit in your car you won't go anywhere. If you start in one direction and then get a better idea, you can easily change your mind and head in another direction. Often the most important learning comes from finding out what you don't like. It is not a mistake to change your direction. It can be a creative adjustment as you move towards the pathway that will be best for you. Persevere until you know the job well and feel clear about what it is you like or don't like. It is brilliant learning when you really dislike something because this leads you to crystal clear thinking about something you will like.

I have known a doctor who chose to become a writer, a mechanic who took up nursing, and an IT specialist who took up aged care work. Make sure you think hard and choose wholeheartedly. It is your journey. Listen to your wants, know your passions and follow them. Use your head to moderate between safe and unrealistic dreams. If you take a pathway that turns out to be not right for you, have the courage to change direction.

Further study or training: battling self-doubt

There is a hard, cold fact that sometimes you have to put up with things you do not enjoy in order to complete a qualification. If you are looking at courses, focus on the bulk of the course and the endpoint of graduation rather than obsessing negatively over the parts of the course that do not appeal to you. Another trap is to think you are not capable of achieving a particular career.

When searching for career options, remember that whenever you take a course you pay good money to institutions to train you. So many times I have heard young people say, 'I could never be a doctor, I wouldn't know what to do'. It is the teacher and the institution's job to teach you everything you need to know to become competent in whatever field.

As long as you complete all the tasks they give you and take the spirit of the training to heart, you will be fine. Make sure you envisage using the skills in the real world rather than just treating them like an assignment that has to be completed. Realise that the tasks they give you have implications for your work in the real world.

I have known students who graduate but discard their career immediately afterwards. They admit that they went through the motions, crammed for exams but never retained information in their head, or imagined what it would be like in the real world. They pass the various subjects, jump through the required hoops and go mindlessly through the course without envisaging themselves actually doing the work in real life. Upon graduation they felt unprepared because they had not tried to integrate what they had learned. They felt like a fake because they had created such a gap between theory and practice.

Make sure you imagine yourself as a real professional as you train. Remember that qualifications and training never produce fully-competent people. They give you a good starting point. Good training will leave you with a feeling that you still have much to learn. Good training will teach you to find a mentor

1. Balancing work, study, relationships, and career aspirations

or a supervisor until you feel competent through experience. Know that it is normal to feel unsure of yourself until you get the experience that allows you to feel competent in your field. It takes years to master a new career. Just go with it!

1.3. Persevering with the option you choose

Once you start, it is exciting to know you are on a pathway to become an expert in your field. Whether you choose an apprenticeship, TAFE, university studies, or some other training course, know that there will be specially-trained teachers to help you. Generally, they have had years of guiding students from Step One to graduation.

Know that there will be times when you feel unmotivated or demoralised. Trust yourself that you can get through the hard stuff. Treat it as something that just has to be done. Don't analyse the value of it. You have chosen your course and have set your end goal, so just push yourself through the tough bits. With any training or course of study the further you get the more opportunity you have to explore areas that really interest you. Whether you enter vocational or academic courses there will be new challenges and opportunities that are different in nature from secondary school. If you fall by the wayside in secondary education there is usually a family member or teacher who will prod you and keep you going. In further study, it is all up to you.

A common trap is allowing your social life to intrude on your study time. Pulling all-nighters, skipping classes, applying for extensions, and cramming for exams are not healthy ways to go. If you see yourself falling into these kinds of traps, know that you must change your priorities quickly. Every time you miss a deadline you will likely prolong the length of your course. For each year you mess up, you will take one year longer to gain the qualifications you need. One year of salary buys a great new car! Oh yes ... and you may have a bigger HECS debt, too!

Unless you plan carefully, your routine can become very confused. Stick to your planned study schedule rather than be thinking about the study you should be doing while you are socialising, or thinking about your social life when you should be studying. This scenario is very inefficient. Work hard and play well.

Organise a study schedule so you still have time for a quota of fun things. Get yourself organised so you can truly enjoy your social life time, as well as the feeling of satisfaction that comes from you putting in good effort. Study when you are scheduled to study and have fun when you have completed your work schedule for the week. Allow yourself a treat at the end of the week if you have stuck to your schedule.

Being well-organised
Map out your study load on a calendar: assignment dates, exam dates, favourite recreational pursuits, family functions, employment commitments, favourite TV programs, time allocation for computer games ... whatever you need to survive! Look at what time you have left. Note down in bright colours your study times. Plan carefully when your study times fall in the week. Your schedule needs to be practical.

The minute you are given assignments or study modules, make sure you have everything you need. Head directly to the library or computer to get your resources. Look at each assessment task and plan out what you have to do. If you are not sure, ASK! You won't become suddenly enlightened by looking at the task over and over. If you don't understand it on first read, then you need clarification from a fellow student or lecturer. The act of 'asking' might require a little perseverance, and lecturers are more likely to be helpful if they have seen you attending their lectures and tutorials.

There is a finite time that you have at your disposal each week. Sporting and creative activities take up varying amounts of time. You might have a consuming passion for one particular activity, but consider the implications on the rest of your life. Does the

1. Balancing work, study, relationships, and career aspirations

time come from your social life or your study commitments? Make sure you apply a sense of balance and order. You might choose to overcommit yourself for a few months for a particular event, and then resume a more balanced set of activities. As long as you have a plan, you will get through.

For instance, if life revolves purely around your ability to play a sport like football or tennis, know that an injury can demolish that lifestyle. The Australian Institute of Sport encourages all athletes to have a backup career plan. Choose a range of hobbies that bring you joy, activities that broaden your social network, and retain contacts to fall back on if life changes for you.

Be cautious of making social media friends whose connection with you is by name only. Far better to have social media connections with the people who have shared in your journey. A friend of a friend does not necessarily constitute friendship for you.

Be wary of newfound friends who have something to gain from you through your friendship. You may want to help them get a job where you work, or help them with a study unit they are stuck on. It is great to have a group of friends who help each other out. However, if the demands keep happening and are largely one way, then you are being used. Remember good friends just enjoy being with you. They don't constantly 'want' from you.

When study doesn't seem relevant
It is hard to focus when you are bored or can't see the point of what you are doing. The first year of tertiary study is often very general and broad in content coverage. It is as if they want you to read every possible article that is related in any way to the subject. It is easy to feel bogged down in things that don't seem relevant to where you want to go.

This is often about providing you with the background you need before you can focus on the detail. It is about broadening your horizons. Go with it! Enjoy the new discoveries and new skills, and all the things you learn on the side while you are working on a topic. As you move through your course you will gradually come to understand why you needed that broad background or basis on which to build your study.

Focus on what is important. Get the hard part over in the most efficient way you can. Rather than agonise over the fact that you really don't want to do it, just accept that you have to do it. Treat it like cleaning your teeth, just another chore that has to be done. Use the thought of your long-term goals to help motivate you to complete the task in front of you.

If you are daydreaming, ask yourself what is consuming your emotional energy. Make a list of the things that worry you. Shelve them until you have finished the task in front of you. Getting into the 'here and now' is the best way to focus. Take control of your brain. Ground yourself by looking around you. Engage your senses in the here and now. If necessary, step outside for a minute and breathe in fresh air. Take a couple of minutes to focus on trees and plants, and feel the sun or the wind on your face. As you walk back inside, ask yourself what you need to do first to engage your head in the first task. Give yourself a time limit to complete the assessment task rather than spending twice the time with half your attention. Make a start!

1.4. Adapting to your new life

It is normal to feel confused, anxious, and wary of suddenly having to think like an adult. You know what the deal is in the school setting. You have heard all the advice, including platitudes about how you should conduct your life, but finally you find yourself in a situation where ... this is it! You are suddenly free to make your own way, to make your own decisions, and to do things the way you choose. This can be both exciting and scary at the same time.

When you leave school you may have to say a goodbye to many of your friends, never knowing in what direction life will take

1. Balancing work, study, relationships, and career aspirations

them or you. While there may still be connection on social media, it is different when geographic distance separates you. Some friends will take up long-term partners you enjoy being around. Others will take partners whose company you really don't care for. Life changes. Even your very best friends will develop new lives, just as you will be doing. The need for new friends is likely to be high on your priority list.

It is important to explore your interests and expand your hobbies. This is a great way to meet new friends with whom you share a common interest. Make sure you put effort into staying in touch with the people you care about. With good friends, the time lapse between connecting is immaterial. You pick up where you left off. The frequency of the connections depends on many things: the distance between you, the strength of the friendship, common interests, study, family and relationship commitments.

In whatever capacity your friendships remain, cherish them, knowing that school friends may not be there for you on a daily basis but may always be part of your life. If you follow your passions and hobbies, new friends will constantly emerge and your friendship group will widen to include a range of new people. Think carefully about your recreational choices and whether they will lead to you broadening your friendship group.

Observe how the friends around you are handling their newfound adult freedom. Some will be making bad choices that will cause ongoing difficulties. Others might be restricting themselves so much that they never move outside their comfort zone. Try to develop new habits, new relationships, and new recreational pursuits that are in line with how you choose to live this phase of your life.

Parents often feel grief over the changes that the next stage of your life will inevitably bring. While you will always remain their child, the relationship changes as you become an adult. Understand that it is a transition for them, as well as you. Be considerate if they are a little overprotective. Tell them that you will let them know if things are not going well. You can reassure them by simply talking through their issues and demonstrating in an adult way that you are capable of making your own wise decisions. For some, this can be a time of extreme selfishness where young people become so swept up in this newfound freedom that they withdraw from conversation with their parents, forgetting to call home until something goes wrong. Others get angry and shut themselves away, refusing to discuss issues. This only makes the situation worse for parents, as well as the young person. It only make things worse.

Think about how you want to handle this transition. Do you really want to be like this? Is this truly what you would want for your parents? Try to talk through differences in a calm way. Show respect for the family and friends who have raised you to be the adult you have become. This is one of the marks of being truly adult.

Be independent and free to have fun. Let loose a little, without going wild. Think about your own journey and trust your own judgement in knowing how you want to handle this transition to total adult freedom. Talk to someone close when you are having difficulties.

Time demands of a partner relationship
While you might have been in a relationship while at school, it is different once you are living an adult life with considerably more freedom and more responsibility. It is pretty easy for your energy to get swept up into a new relationship. Like too much sport, too much study, too much lazing around, or too much of anything, it throws the rest of life out of balance. Pushing away good friends in order to spend time in the new relationship is a risky thing to do. People don't like being pushed aside. That friend you meet for coffee every week will resent being ditched just because you have a new partner. Think carefully about how you treat your friends at this time when the blush of new love is on you.

1. Balancing work, study, relationships, and career aspirations

It is possible that a relationship at this stage of your life might turn out to be the one that lasts a lifetime. It is also possible that you will have several relationships before you settle with someone as a lifetime commitment, making your current relationship just a temporary one. If this happens, it will be extremely helpful to have your friends around you. If you have pushed them away, you might find yourself without friends. Think about how your friends are travelling. Consider their ups and downs and return the friendship when things go wrong for them. Friendships may last forever, whereas relationships sometimes do not.

While you might want to spend every available minute with this new partner, the rest of your life has to go on if you are going to achieve your goals. Talk about these things. Talk about how you can both have interesting and active lives away from each other, alongside special time together. A healthy relationship is where each partner easily moves in and out of the relationship in order to lead individual lives. This is done thoughtfully and with respect.

It is easier to give each other space if you both have the capacity to be 100% emotionally present in the times when you are together. It will also help if you are thoughtful, kind, and put effort into staying connected amidst your busy schedule. Kindness and caring really only takes a few seconds of thoughtful communication. You can each do that. Being too busy for a 30-second phone call may be an occasional reality, but is not an acceptable five-day excuse.

If this is your partner, step back and reassess the give and take nature of your relationship. Reflect on whether you are being too needy, or your partner is being inconsiderate. A strong relationship will sustain time apart. Strong relationships allow for an ebb and flow, for easy connections flowing in and outside the relationship. There has to be balance between independence and interdependence, often called enmeshment.

If your partner needs you to be there emotionally for them 24/7 then try to work out if your partner is just going through an unexpected difficult time, or if they are generally needy. A relationship that totally enmeshes you in your partner's world is not healthy. There is a difference between *wanting* to be with someone and *needing* to be with someone. In its extreme, the latter shows a lack of respect for your wellbeing. Emotional blackmail is very devious and can be very destructive. I have known many a young adult who has fallen in love and given their all, only to find that a year later they have dropped out of their course and their relationship has fallen through.

It is worth taking stock of your part in the relationship. Ask yourself if you are being overly self-centred. Are you only prepared to see this special person when it suits you? There has to be give and take in any relationship. Commitments and demands on your time need to be explained and discussed.

Relationships are easily blown apart by disrespectful or thoughtless behaviour. Call when you say you will call. Be on time when you arrange to meet someone. Build trust, rather than break it down. Trust is easily lost and hard to regain. On a flight to Singapore I saw a delightful advertisement about a young man bringing his young love home on time, arriving at the family's door at 11.00pm. Fearful of the reaction in case he might be 30 seconds late, he was finally greeted with an approving smile from the father. The caption was, 'Trust is a one-time gift'.

Be trustworthy and honourable! Trust can only be built bit by bit when there is a strong foundation of love. When a relationship is new, one seed of doubt leads to insecurity and potential relationship destruction. Every moment in a relationship counts, especially the 'moments of truth' that speak louder than relationship history. Forgetting that critical event or not being there for something close to your partner's heart can result in your partner losing respect for you. It might turn out to be a deal-breaker.

Before choosing to go into a serious relationship, you and your partner need to be sure about the kind of commitment you want and expect. Your goals and dreams need to be talked about, along with the impact they will likely have on both your lives. Try to be solid in your independence as well as being able to enjoy being and giving to a special someone. This is very different from being with someone because of what you want or need from them.

1.5. If life feels like it is falling apart

It is really important to acknowledge and celebrate your successes. However, it is unrealistic to expect to be happy all the time. Life throws out curveballs. Living involves many thousands of emotions experienced alongside your adventures. To live means to have ups and downs, good times, bad times, fantastic times, and horrible times.

When there are things that upset you in several areas of life it is normal to feel overwhelmed. Life happens that way sometimes, and the sense of powerlessness can feel paralysing. It is normal to feel like your life is falling apart. Most people feel like this at some point in their life, but know that it is a temporary feeling. Reassure yourself that it is okay, that you can get through it, and that you will get through it.

When everything seems to be going wrong it is common for people to leap into their head to try to solve the situation. We have all been taught to think things through, to think sensibly, problem solve, work it out, use our brain, etc. This is helpful in straightforward situations. It is not helpful when there is a level of complexity and no easy answer. It produces a lot of rumination (repetitive thinking). If you focus so much on your head and get lost in the thoughts that merely go round and round, you enter a state of overthinking. In this state you are likely to work yourself into a high state of anxiety and lose the capacity to think clearly. It is possible to hear voices if you are highly anxious, and you can feel like you are losing control of your brain.

If this ever happens to you, calm yourself, breathe in large volumes of air, and slowly exhale. Try patterned breathing:

four in, four out. Ground yourself and use your senses to get into the here and now. When there are many possible pathways to solutions, it often comes down to choosing the pathway that feels right for you. If you are feeling anxious and unhappy, take time to reassess your life and ask yourself what has been missing for you. If you can identify the things that make you really unhappy then you can analyse the reasons and explore new pathways.

Learn to drop into your emotional self and ask yourself, firstly, what you need to do in the short-term to sort yourself out. Do you need time out? Do you want to be with a loved one? Do you want time to sit and cry? Do you want to leave a certain situation? Do you want to have a new start? Do you need time with good friends? Do you need a new experience or a new physical challenge? Questions for your heart will bring you more answers than overthinking everything.

Secondly, when you have taken the pressure off yourself, ask yourself honestly what it is that you want, or what it is that you want to change. Staying in your head won't help you get to this point. You have to know what you want before you can make a good decision. Match your feelings with the values and principles you hold in your head. These are the beliefs about living that you hold strong in your mind, and also agree with in your heart. Is there a good match, or do they contradict each other? Do you have a green light on your pathway, or a stop sign?

Remember, a little bit of logical thinking will always help you manage your life, but locking yourself into logical thinking is likely to sap you emotionally and paralyse you physically. You become unable to take action because you have so many opposing thoughts. Anxiety traps you into a frenetic state that stops your ability to think well. It is like studying for exams. If you are in a high state of anxiety over failing, you brain has no capacity left to perform in the exam. Free your brain by calming yourself. You can push through anything if you want it enough, so focus on the power of knowing what you want.

1. Balancing work, study, relationships, and career aspirations

If you are still struggling with complexity of thought, set your ideas for various solutions down on paper, like a map. Circle the areas of your life that are most important. Add a word to describe your feelings about each solution. It is so much easier to write complex things onto paper than hold them in your head. Look at one area at a time. How important is it to you that there is change in each area? Note what you think you will lose and what you will gain. Think about how you might be feeling when you have made a change in your chosen direction.

You will then need to make some gutsy decisions to shape your future. Plan the actions you need to take. Follow your heart and start putting the building blocks in place to gradually build the kind of future you would like. Be confident that you can do it!

Remember that if you are feeling down, it is only temporary. With a little analysis and effort on your part you will be able to work out something that will put you in a better place. You might soon be in a situation where every part of your life is happy, and maybe even exciting beyond what you can currently imagine. You will be able to work through it, towards the choices and decisions open to you. Out of bad situations often come brilliant futures. Out of catastrophic situations come new priorities and hidden gifts.

Help yourself to feel better. Get some exercise, take some time out in the environment. Get out of the surrounds of your bedroom and computer and go outside, without your social media devices, and be in the real world for a while. While you are out there, calm yourself and really focus on what you need to do to get yourself back on track.

2

Building employment prospects

2.1. Starting work

2.2. Having fun and building a good reputation at work

2.3. Dating in the workplace

2.4. Interpersonal dynamics in the workplace

2.5. Knowing your rights in the workplace

2.1. Starting work

With any job interview, make sure you look smart. Try a little colour on you such as a shirt, tie, scarf, necklace, or something that stands out and makes you look bright and cheery. Rehearse the interview in your head; perhaps even make a video of yourself answering some questions. This will give you an idea of how the interviewer might see you. Be ready for some direct, businesslike questions. Before you go to the interview, write down on a small piece of paper all the questions you need to ask, e.g. starting date, hours, rate of pay, location, parking and who you would report to.

Include a couple of questions pertinent to the organisation, e.g. what other outlets does the organisation have, is the business planning any new ventures? Read up on whatever you can when you are away from the business so you have something to ask. At the interview, be candid about your strengths. For instance, you might say that you are reliable and responsible, and have been praised often for your initiative. Give your potential new employer confidence that you will be a worthwhile employee.

If you miss out on the job, rather than waste time and emotional energy beating yourself up, do a quick assessment of your own performance at the interview. It does not necessarily mean that you performed badly at the interview. There may have been good applicants who have extensive experience. If you made some mistakes then you can learn from these. It is perfectly acceptable to ring the job interviewer and ask for feedback. While you may simply get feedback saying there were lots of applicants, it is worth making the phone call to see if they can give you any other valuable information.

You will eventually find work. The more interviews you have the more interview experience you will gain. Be industrious about talking to your friends and family networks. Let everyone know you are keen and something will turn up. The first job is the hardest. With future jobs, you will be a person who has work experience, something that is rated highly by employers.

If you are lucky enough to gain employment quickly, take things one step at a time. Listen carefully, follow instructions, and ask for clarification if you are not sure. If you are feeling a little nervous, just say to yourself, 'It is to be expected', and then push that feeling aside. You will soon be seen as a good employee if you are prepared to listen, ask and learn, work hard, and are punctual.

It is natural to feel a little strange and lacking in confidence when you start anything new. Know that it is normal to feel this way. If you seriously start to doubt your capabilities, remember that good employers provide systematic training, support, and encouragement. If you bring a happy disposition to the workplace you will be appreciated. As you gain confidence you will become quicker at everything. Your boss and your co-workers will get to know you, and no doubt come to enjoy many of your special qualities.

As you settle in, you may have insights that others don't have. How you manage those insights will define how you will be regarded. Be careful never to criticise a fellow worker or boss behind their back. Keep negative comments to yourself and your trusted friends outside work. If you have a suggestion, put it to your supervisor in a way that is respectful. Say something like, 'What would you think about doing [X] this way?' or, 'I don't know if this is a crazy idea but what if ...'

Always remember that, regardless of age or experience, your manager should be treated with respect. If you find you are placed under a manager just a few years older or younger than yourself, make sure you show that manager respect. If you are pressed to give feedback, make sure you do it in a way that makes positive suggestion, rather than negative criticism. Frame it in a way that demonstrates your idea will make the process more productive or ease the burden, or will be profitable. There is an art to doing this, and it is worth mastering.

In the workplace, remember that respect has to be shown to your colleagues and your supervisors. It is immaterial whether or not you like them. Your manager should also treat you with dignity and respect.

2.2. Having fun and building a good reputation at work

Workplaces can be lots of fun. When you get a group of people working together who get on well with each other, the workplace can be a very validating and enjoyable place to be. Like all participants, you have the capacity to contribute to the social environment. You make a negative contribution when you bring your home or study difficulties into work in the form of a poor mood. If there is a person or a group of people you really don't like and you develop a real 'set' against them, your contribution will be negative. It is so important to put these feelings aside and to treat everyone in a friendly and respectful way.

Every member of the team has their own story. Whether or not you like them or they like you, you have to treat people with respect and have pleasant social interchange. Say hello to everyone you meet as you come in the door. Simple things like offering a coffee as you get yours, or holding the lift for someone are the kinds of things that demonstrate goodwill. While you may have different intellectual ideas about your work, this sort of behaviour shows that you still have the capacity to treat people as human beings and show them respect.

It is not just employers who you need to get along with. Poor behaviour towards another workmate will quickly become the topic of discussion behind closed doors. Your employer will soon get the picture if you are a different person amongst your peers. On the other hand, if you are prepared to 'go the extra mile' you will be highly regarded. If you are respectful to every person in the organisation, regardless of their job, people will start to trust you as a decent person, one who is prepared to do the right thing. If you are rude to those on a lower wage than you, you will find that your bad reputation will permeate your social circles at work.

Remember, while you may voice your own opinions at home, at work you need to contribute positively to the environment. What happens over time is that you build a good reputation as an honourable employee, and this reputation will follow you wherever you go. It will be a consistent theme in the words of referees and word-of-mouth recommendations. It may be the main factor in getting you your next job. Every additional responsibility you take on is fuel for your resume. If, on the other hand, you speak your mind and behave like a smartarse towards those you don't like, you will be seen as arrogant and rude. If you wish to be regarded as having integrity, then your words must match your actions, regardless of the situation. You can't say one thing to a person's face and another behind their back.

While casual work definitely has benefits, monitoring your own energy levels and your ability to juggle commitments is critical. Casual work can be tiring, and can disrupt your study if you are frequently called in for extra shifts. Employers can be unfairly demanding of your time, and this can affect your ability to study. Time for relaxation is important. Most people have to work to earn a living, so it is great if you love your work because it makes the time pass by quickly. Once work consumes your every day, then life outside work diminishes. Balance is always the key. Politely refuse if your employer is wanting too much of your time, and explain why. Tell them that you are already feeling overstretched across your commitments, and you would not like to let the organisation down in a big way if you crash and become ill.

Enjoy learning to get along with people from other backgrounds. Seek out things to learn from them. It can be fun and enriching as you make contacts for life, and generally broaden your experience of the world. Enjoy putting other people at ease by chatting to them. Join in any of the fun activities that happen in your workplace. Be on the lookout for those who are having a rough time. A friendly gesture will change their experience. Be ready for a bit of a laugh. Tell others something you appreciate about them. Remember that this group is just made up of ordinary people who are keen to learn, and to contribute something to society in general. They have the same fears, worries, and self-doubts. Relax and just be yourself, keen and eager to learn. You will have fun!

Fighting off a crisis of confidence

I think most adults have had the experience of feeling not good enough at some time in their lives. If this feeling strikes you, it is important to work out where it has come from. Are you feeling uncertain? Do you feel you can do your job efficiently? Do you need more training? Are you struggling with getting to work on time? Are you struggling to fit everything into your life? Are you being bullied? Is someone doing a power trip on you? There can be a multitude of reasons contributing to a feeling of lost confidence, and it usually comes from criticism by others. If you are really concerned, ask your supervisor for direct feedback.

If you are not doing so well and the contributing factors are largely to do with you and your lifestyle, then that is easy to fix. Have the courage to admit to yourself the things you need to change, and then set about changing them. If the contributing factors are largely to do with the work environment, remember it is your employer's job to train you adequately, to treat you with respect, and to preserve your dignity when you do make a mistake. It is your employer's job to be clear about what is needed from you. If what your employer tells you does not make sense to you, make sure you ask for clarification. Look around for another person who might be able help you understand.

At the end of the day, you need to walk out the door knowing you have put in good effort and have conscientiously tried to take everything in and learn from your mistakes. Remember, mistakes are to be expected. It will get easier over time. If something doesn't feel right and you are feeling demeaned or bullied then you need to realise that you are not the one with the problem.

There is major lifelong learning in all of the above. Reflect on your own weaknesses and do something about them. Reflect on whether or not you are avoiding taking responsibility for your mistakes or refusing to learn from them. Make sure you also reflect on your employer's part in the situation. What I can't say strongly enough is, for the rest of your working life, NEVER, EVER allow poor management or poor organisational culture to diminish your confidence or your self-esteem! Too often I have seen competent young people in all kinds of occupations and levels who suffer a self-esteem battering because their supervisor or manager lacks good management skills.

2.3. Dating in the workplace

It is well-known that people often meet their future spouse at work. Shared interests and shared talents often present interesting relationships. If your new relationship involves a close co-worker, tread gently. Consider the risk if something goes wrong.

In regular social circles dating often goes wrong as new relationships take a dive and ultimately cease. Couples find out that they do not mesh well in a number of aspects of their personality, beliefs, sexuality or lifestyle. It is a part of the natural sifting and sorting to find the relationship that will stand the test of time.

If this happens with someone you work closely with the repercussions can be difficult because it is impossible to avoid seeing the ex-partner on a daily basis. Breakups do not always go smoothly. Not everyone is honourable. Not everyone is mature enough to handle a breakup in a respectful way. Hurt and bitterness can lead some people to become very nasty. They can lash out, hurt, or demean the ex-partner for instigating the breakup. They can make up vindictive lies to save face.

If you engage in a relationship between you and your supervisor or manager, the legal and ethical situation becomes extremely tricky. I have seen many times that it can bring about dismissal for one, or both. There can also be unfair allegations of bullying or harassment. When relationships sour, the previously happy workplace can turn into a dreaded place to go, with one partner choosing to leave, usually the employee. The risks and the stakes are high if the relationship does not work out. Even if it does, the workplace can become unpleasant as other staff members imagine favouritism. For all these reasons, many adults have a policy of never dating workmates. It is always safer to keep dating relationships away from the workplace. If a relationship is meant to be it can be nurtured gradually, and it can wait till one of you can move to a more distant work location.

2.4. Interpersonal dynamics in the workplace

Workplace games
While most people behave pleasantly in the workplace, there is always a small number of personalities with whom you need to be circumspect; for instance, employees who play power

games or try to make you look bad through deception and dishonest tricks. This is, of course, unacceptable. It is bullying. It is a small chance, but if this happens to you, remind yourself that you have so little respect for this person that it is not worth wasting your energy on them.

Maintain your own dignity and don't lower yourself to the other person's bad behaviour. This is critical. A tricky part of their power play can be to get you to behave badly, then be ready to drop you into bad consequences. More than likely, it will have nothing to do with you personally. People have their own agendas for their behaviour. It could be something like an irrational fear that they hold that you will be after their job so they need to move you on. If someone bullies you in this way, be smart and keep your reactions private. Go home and talk it through with someone. Think smart about collecting evidence and planning strategies to deal with the situation. This will produce a much more positive outcome than retaliating in kind with poor behaviour. Take positive and appropriate action through respectable channels.

As you quietly and calmly collect evidence, take note of who else might have seen or heard the situation play out. Write it down, date it, sign it, and get it witnessed. If there is a problem of any kind, start documenting straight away. You might then let the abusive person know that you are ready to report inappropriate behaviour if it happens again. Be patient. This person is bound to trip themselves up sooner or later, with you or another person. You have your statement at home and ready to go!

If your employer wants to pay you slightly higher wages without taking any tax, or paying super for you, be very cautious how you handle the situation. Simply state that you would prefer payment in the regular way with tax and super taken out. It is illegal and not in your interests to accept wages 'under the table'.

Other subtle games include employees who always try to make themselves look good to their employer at the expense of their co-workers. It astounds me to see how often some people believe it is okay to take a great idea from someone else and run with it as if it was their own. Common decency means that you acknowledge when an ideas has come from someone else. This kind of attitude is always appreciated by employers.

Bullying in the workplace

Workplaces require that everyone pitch in and help when things get busy. Because of this, it is important not to be too precious. This means that you are able to take a bit of a joke, laugh, and enjoy some social banter. If you are unsure whether this is what is going on in your workplace or whether you are being harassed, look to your feelings and ask yourself the question, 'Is this person intentionally setting out to hurt me or to make me feel inferior?' If so, then start documenting everything that is said or done, including the date, time, and witnesses to each incident.

The following bullying behaviours are examples of unacceptable behaviour in the workplace:

- Being yelled at, or having blatant rude remarks or offensive language screamed at you.
- Deliberately not passing on the information you require to do your job (for example, withholding the roster).
- Socially isolating you or not including you in work-organised social activities.
- Put-downs, demeaning remarks, nicknames that offend or patronise.
- Deliberately giving incorrect instructions, information, or impossible tasks.
- Blackmail of any kind.

If you experience anything similar to the above, it's important to seek help. Identify who you can take the issue to. Can you take it to your immediate manager, or a manager higher up the chain? If necessary, report to fair work authorities. There is government legislation in place to protect you from bullying. You need documentation and evidence for any formal process.

Bullying behaviour has to be reported if it is to change. Understand that employers have a responsibility to train you, and a right to discipline you. They also have a right to give firm directions about how work is to be carried out. At the same time, while employers have the right to performance manage you, they are also expected to give you constructive feedback and guidance on how to improve your participation. Balance is required. It is not helpful to be so overly precious that you can't take a joke made purely in fun. On the other hand, it is foolish to put up with behaviour that is motivated by a need to bully.

If you are finding your boss difficult to deal with

It is always in your best interest to inspire confidence in your boss with regards to your ability. Before you determine your boss to be 'difficult', take careful stock of whether you have done anything rude, inappropriate, careless, dishonest, or disrespectful. If so, then take responsibility to fix up the situation. Forgive yourself for stuffing up and resolve to do better. Apologise to him or her with an undertaking to work on it. When you show humility it goes a long way to repairing a situation. If, on the other hand, you deny any responsibility or blame someone else, it paves the pathway for a downhill slide in the eyes of your boss.

Be very quick to apologise if you think you have messed something up. Remember, everyone makes mistakes. The bigger the mistake, the more you are likely to learn. The important thing is that you make sure you don't make the same mistake over and over. Remember, there are more parts to an apology than the word sorry. You need to mean it. You need to acknowledge what you did, and then you need to set about making things as right as you possibly can. If you find you are continuing to make the same mistakes, then maybe your heart is not truly in the job. Treat each day as a new day, and make sure you smile and greet your employer and your colleagues with a, 'Good morning' or 'Good evening' to show that you have moved on from any bad feelings.

If you are confident that you have done nothing wrong, and don't deserve the criticism you just received, hold back your reaction. Go on conscientiously with your daily work and wait for the opportunity to state your case. Maybe that will be at the end of the day on your own time when you can quietly say, 'I need to let you know that the situation was not what you think it was, and I would like two minutes of your time to explain'.

Any reasonable boss will give you time to explain. If your employer is not prepared to do this then the best you can hope for is that the conflict will just blow over with time. If your employer continues to treat you badly, then you have two choices:

The first is to accept emotionally that you have a very difficult boss for whom you hold little regard. This first option frees you to be able to let the criticism flow over your head. It requires that you acknowledge internally that your boss is the one with the problem, and it requires that you learn to ignore their tone or sarcasm as you go about your work. Externally, you have to be pleasant and do what is asked of you without showing resentment. This option is suitable if you need to hang onto your job because the income you get from it is more important than your enjoyment of the job. You might start carefully planning for a job change.

The only other choice might be to resign and look for another job straight away. Discuss this with friends or family who know your situation. They might have other suggestions as to how to make your employer back off and appreciate what you do. Casual work might be hard work, but it should also be pleasant. Remember, you have a right not to be bullied. At the very least you should expect to be treated with respect, rather than humiliation.

2.5. Knowing your rights in the workplace

Most people find workplaces to be fair and equitable places, so it is unlucky if you find yourself in a workplace with a bullying culture. Some general knowledge about procedures will never go astray. It might assist you, or one of your friends.

Firstly, remember that an accusation made with no respect for the truth or your reputation falls under the description of slander/discrimination. Secondly, understand that assault does not have to be physical. If you or your colleague are fearful that you are in danger then this constitutes assault. Thirdly, it is good general knowledge to know that if someone needs to report assault or harassment then they should have a witness or support person present in any formal meeting. Similarly, anyone accused of doing the wrong thing should also take a witness or a support person to any consultation with the employer. Fourth, there are avenues through Fair Work to gain support for award conditions.

Prepare carefully if you have to attend a formal meeting. Make a record of events and facts surrounding the situation. At the time of the meeting, insist on a private room rather a room in hearing of other workers. Be clear about what you know. Present the facts simply and concisely. Stay calm and determined. Stand your ground on what is true! Be prepared to compromise on differences of opinion without being a doormat. State what you believe, acknowledge the difference of opinion, and say what compromise you are prepared to make.

When there is an accusation of sexual harassment or assault, it is standard practice that the harasser be interviewed in a different room to the target of the harassment. After the interviews, each party leaves separately with a time gap in between. Note that suspension of employment without pay is not usually permitted by law. If you find yourself in this kind of situation, make sure you contact your union for support.

3
Nurturing yourself

3.1. *Looking after your self-esteem and building resilience*

3.2. *Identifying the mental scripts that constrain you*

3.3. *Comparing yourself to others*

3.4. *Being bold – making yourself heard*

3.5. *Burnout*

3.6. *Overcoming stress, overthinking and anxiety*

3.7. *Dealing with depression*

3.8. *Coping with loss*

3.1. Looking after your self-esteem and building resilience

It is important to make choices that will help you feel good about yourself and build your self-esteem. The internal dialogue you use is important. If you constantly say to yourself, 'I am so, so stupid,' you are assaulting your own self-esteem over and over. When things go wrong you will probably be less resilient because you will lack belief in yourself. On the other hand, if your internal dialogue is positive you will be more likely to keep trying. You will analyse your mistakes, learn from them, and try again. You will be more resilient.

It is important to protect and guard your self-esteem from others as well as yourself. Take in a big deep breath and try again. Be determined to achieve the end goal rather than cave in because your confidence is low over one small mistake. Keep track of your feelings. Talk to someone if you are getting overwhelmed by lots of negative emotion. Be prepared to express feelings of disappointment and hurt, but be quick to say to yourself that you won't be defeated, that you believe in yourself and you won't take any notice of negative self-talk.

When you express your feelings, you move through them
It is curious that so many people guard their feelings at all costs, yet feel confident in throwing forward all their ideas for public scrutiny. People will go to great lengths to avoid expressing their feelings. They expect emotional hurt to be over in two days, though they know a broken bone takes months. They feel quite panicky when the emotional hurt does not resolve quickly, losing patience with themselves. One thing is for sure; if you hold on to emotional pain, it lingers forever. Alternatively, if you express what hurts, the pain lifts. You have to trust this process and be brave enough to choose a trusted person to talk to.

I am constantly suggesting to clients that they need not be so afraid of expressing their feelings. Feelings need to be treasured like gold. Once expressed, they can't be taken away. They are yours and they can't be debated. I suggest that when you offer your feelings to someone else, you give them a gift of 'yourself'. Your feelings just *are*. They may not be logical, rational, appropriate, reasonable, or politically correct, and may not meet with approval. However, they are real and very different to ideas that can be disputed endlessly.

I have known people so terrified of falling apart and having a cry that they will walk out of a marriage rather than express their feelings. I have known people who will shy away from therapy because they fear it might diminish their ability to function in their day-to-day world. They imagine that if they let one feeling out the rest will follow, and they will unable to control the flood of emotion. Suicidal ideation for some is preferable to expressing emotion in the presence of another, and yet those who have expressed that kind of fear and have gone through with a therapy session say that this kind of fear had been unfounded. They openly acknowledge that their first ever counselling session was the best thing they ever did.

Some people understand instinctively that once you have expressed your feelings you move through them to a different emotional place. It is not healthy to hold onto intense emotion. This causes stress and ill health and often stops you from getting what you need to be happy. How sad it is that our society still encultures young men into thinking they are not real men if they shed a tear? While emotional expression is now acceptable on the football field, many young men still feel it is not acceptable in the home, or the counselling room.

When you are consumed by a strong emotion that you know is out of context with your situation, it may be that the particular cluster of emotions you are experiencing is similar to something you experienced in the past, maybe even in childhood. For instance, a grown adult might find themselves panicking at the sight of a clown for no apparent reason. What the adult is likely to report is a sense of craziness because, being a grown person, there is no logical reason to feel fearful of the clown. And yet, in an emotional sense this person has slipped down the slippery slide back to a time when they really feared clowns. When this happens, you suddenly find yourself behaving like a child or the way you reacted in the original fearful situation. It is as if you are reliving an earlier, often traumatic experience.

Therapy helps you identify the cause of over-the-top emotional reactions. Once light is shone on the origins of the trigger, you will likely experience an 'ah-ha' moment. This then allows you to cope much better in the current situations that cause you distress. By talking about what you feel, you will come to understand your emotions better. It will all begin to make sense.

Know that when you express what you feel, you move to a different understanding of your situation. The reality of the words you use can have an impact on you as you speak them. In verbalising your thoughts and feelings, they may become more real to you. You might feel more validated or have greater understanding of exactly how you really feel. Yes, this might seem a little unsettling at first, but it will help you to clarify the issues, to move on and take some kind of action to effect the change that you need to relieve your current emotional pain. Find someone you trust to hold your confidence. It might also help to express your emotion in any other way that feels right for you, whether it be writing, dancing, painting, or any other kind of expressive art.

Change is inevitable, both within ourselves, and from external sources. By acknowledging you are in a period of transition you will be able to reduce the expectations on yourself to get it all together. You are more likely to become stuck if you panic and assume you will stay unhappy forever. Denial of your feelings and shutting yourself off from them keeps you stuck, where you experience them over and over again. Movement through emotional states flows more easily once you begin to express what you are feeling.

3.2. Identifying the mental scripts that constrain you

We all have stories that we run over and over again like a well-rehearsed script. They are patterns of thinking that follow us through life and influence our actions. They often sit just on the edge of our awareness. Sometimes they are helpful, sometimes they are destructive. A script that tells you not to go to bed without cleaning your teeth is helpful. However, negative scripts that replay in your mind can seriously affect the way

3. Nurturing yourself

you live. These stories are old beliefs that have become routine and are applied automatically, often beyond your awareness. They can also be so sufficiently in your awareness that you overcompensate for them or apply them in situations where they are really not relevant. In this way, the long held belief is caught up in patterns of feeling and behaving. You might find yourself carrying out the old patterns over and over without really understanding why.

For instance:

> *'I'm entitled to that!'*
>
> *'I might be left alone if I let this friend go.'*
>
> *'It's not fair, I never get what I want.'*
>
> *'I need someone to tell me what to do.'*
>
> *'What if I am not needed anymore?'*
>
> *'This will be disaster.'*
>
> *'People are always taking advantage of me.'*
>
> *'I am not lovable.'*
>
> *'I can never belong, I am different.'*
>
> *'I am not very clever, I am a real fake.'*
>
> *'I am not good enough.'*

If you truly believe the 'I am unlovable' script, you may overcompensate by avoiding relationships or by seeking lots of relationships. You might try to prove you are lovable by staying in a bad relationship. If you are sucked in by the 'I am not good enough' script, you might avoid challenges or be burdened with a lack of confidence. Sadly, in this scenario you would miss the sense of satisfaction that could come from your achievements.

The emotional connection to these kinds of old scripts can be quite intense and make it really hard to let go of them. Some feel shame in finding it so hard to let go of these out of date behaviours, especially if their script is around feeling like a failure. Try to take note of your own personal scripts and identify the impact they might be having on your life. Most scripts come from a time in the past where they served some survival purpose (e.g. if I keep quiet I won't get into trouble, or if I keep to myself I won't get hurt again, or pride comes before a fall so I must not feel good about my success).

In adulthood these scripts are past their use-by date. As an adult you have many more skills and resources to deal with difficult situations than in your youth. If you can identify any common scripts popping into your awareness, you can then analyse the current evidence against them. You may find it is time to reframe them into something that is more useful, and truer now. For instance, 'I am an adult now and I am confident in having a go at anything new', or 'I have had good relationships with people and have experienced being lovable', or 'it is good to feel proud of my effort as long as I am not gloating or being arrogant'. Once you apply a new script, you will find your life will change.

3.3. Comparing yourself to others

As a young adult embarking on new study pathways, new job, or new career, it is very tempting to look around and compare yourself to others. Going from a small school to a large TAFE or university campus puts you in touch with hundreds of very talented young people. It can feel quite overwhelming at first, before you start to realise that they are all feeling just as insecure about finding their place in this new environment. Trust that your education has equipped you to handle whatever is required. Enjoy the thousands of personalities you will meet. It won't take long to find your own group of friends with whom you feel comfortable and relaxed.

3. Nurturing yourself

If you feel overawed by those you meet, be aware that for many people their greatest strengths are often their greatest weaknesses. For instance, someone who is academically able may have difficulty with practical skills. A highly artistic person may have difficulty organising themselves. A highly social person may have difficulty withdrawing enough to meet work deadlines. You will never know the life stories of other people unless they openly and honestly confide in you. When someone appears to be perfect on the outside, on the inside this may not be the case. To imagine they are so much better than you is to see only one aspect of their lives. If you find yourself doing this, ask yourself what it is you admire, and seek to build that attribute in yourself, but never assume according to your imagination.

Trust that you are okay as you are. With goals in mind you can balance hard work and a rewarding social life. When you find yourself comparing yourself to others, remember that they have skills and talents that you aspire to (if that is really important to you) but they will also have flaws and negative aspects to their personalities. Focus on a realistic view of people, rather than be tricked by your imagination that these other people are in some way perfect. They are not! I have never met a perfect human being. Everyone has flaws in their personality. That is what makes us uniquely human. Wasting emotional energy trying to be someone you are not is counterproductive. Once you accept yourself with all your strengths and weaknesses, you can put your energy into harnessing those strengths and trying to overcome the weaknesses.

Keep your goals in mind, and while you take time to celebrate the effort you put into your successes, be careful not to be defined by them. Life is full of disappointments, as well as joyous moments. Failing, succeeding, and meeting challenges are all part of life and learning. None of them define you. You are more than the sum of all your strivings. You are more than the sum of your failures or successes. With all the messes that happen while living, your journey will pass through them like a train journey that goes through dark tunnels and open clearings. The scenery is all part of the trip.

3.4. Being bold – making yourself heard

Some people try to make themselves heard by shouting others down or belittling their ideas. In the heat of an argument people often confuse facts with opinions and insist on being right. The best way to make yourself heard is to stay calm and speak up. Say honestly what you think, feel, and prefer. This is an assertive model that gives you authenticity.

Being assertive means putting yourself into the situation. If you own what you say, for example, 'I think', 'I feel', and 'I prefer', others can't take offence. This is very different from finger pointing and saying things in a way that demeans another person's opinion. This is what people experience if you use the word 'You' during your interaction, e.g. 'You are wrong' will produce more hostility than 'I think differently'. Make yourself heard in an assertive rather than a judgemental or aggressive way. If you are authentic and well intentioned, others will listen to you. If you act in accordance with what you say, then others will see you as a person with integrity.

If you are ever asked to give a talk, do it in a way that will make others want to listen to what you are saying. Pay attention to how you speak, and how you use facial expressions or hand movements. If you mutter quietly with your head down others won't hear you at all. Hold your head up, make good eye contact, and speak out. Take note of the register in your voice, whether it sounds like you are talking too high, or through your nose, or whether you are speaking from a full chest. The timbre of your voice needs to be a smooth sound that makes it easy to listen to.

There is nothing more boring than a monotone delivery where every sentence and phrase sounds the same. Try to emphasise the important things, vary your voice, and slow the pace down. Give people time to think. Allow some moments when you don't speak at all. Pause for effect. Be loud enough for everyone to hear, but vary the loudness according to the importance of what you are saying.

Practise being confident

If you think you need to wait till you are master of your world in order to feel confident, it will never happen. Confidence is a way of thinking. It focuses on what you are doing, not what you are. It reflects a belief that you can meet challenges and overcome difficulties. It is about the journey, and not the destination. It is about believing in yourself.

When you make your case to others, act confidently. For instance, you will not feel or appear confident if, on meeting someone for the first time, you lower your eyes and hesitantly hold your hand out to shake theirs. Your thoughts will be a self-fulfilling prophesy. If, on the other hand, you stand up straight, make direct eye contact, and boldly hold your hand out to give a firm handshake, you will feel confident. You will 'be' confident!

If you want to be confident in a particular area, do your research so you know what you are talking about. Being confident with a particular topic requires dedication and perseverance. It means not giving up till you feel knowledgeable on the topic. It is normal to yearn for more confidence when you lack experience or when you learn a new skill. The first time you rode a bike you were not only wobbly on it, but maybe wobbly in your self-confidence. With practice you became more confident. If you don't prompt yourself to develop mental confidence you won't ever get on the bike.

When your confidence is wavering because you have been involved in a difficult conflict, think logically about what has happened. Are you beating yourself up over the way it played out, or are you angry with the other party? In this situation what you have to master is the ability to be balanced in your outlook. This is easy when the issue is mild. It is easy to step back and identify your part in the issue, and what you need to assign to other people or to unfortunate situations. In crisis situations, it is too easy to slip down into old habitual ways of thinking. Self-blamers quickly beat themselves up and feel responsible for everything. External blamers quickly refuse to take responsibility for anything. Neither response is healthy. If you find yourself responding in either fashion, bring yourself to the middle. Calmly sort out the bit you truly need to take responsibility for, and what you need to recognise as outside your control – the part you need to push back, the part that others need to take responsibility for.

In any new work situation it takes time and experience to develop expertise. You may define yourself as a rookie at the moment, but as the months pass and you gain experience you will no longer be that. We all grow enormously and change in different ways. How you define yourself today will not be how you see yourself in the future. That old rookie feeling will become just a faint memory. If you keep reflecting on where and how you want to grow, the change in you will be intentional, rather than haphazard or simply a reaction to external events.

When you take a new course of study, it is normal to feel a lack of true confidence with new tasks. It is the job of those instructing you to pass on their knowledge in such a way that you learn the necessary skills, and ultimately master them. There is no point in saying I can't be a nurse because I wouldn't know how to look after sick people. It is the job of the instructors to teach you that. As long as you are open to learning and study you will achieve the mastery required. Act confidently. Say to yourself, 'I've never done this before but I can give it a go! If I fail I will learn something, and I'll make sure I will do better second time around'. Follow up with something like, 'Who cares what those around me think? I know where I am going with this. I probably won't even remember the name of the person beside me 10 years from now'. Use whatever comes to mind to boost your confidence level.

Life is a continual experience of new situations. If you acknowledge to yourself that you intend to do your best, that you intend to behave in appropriate ways, and that mistakes are inevitable because you are human, then you have every reason to act confidently. The more confidently you act, the more truly confident you will become. Being confident means being open to new opportunities, open to new ideas, and believing in yourself.

3.5. Burnout

If you throw yourself into work or study and fail to take time out for relaxation and connecting with others, you might find that you start to suffer from burnout. I am not talking about a fleeting, day-long feeling, or a temporary lack of motivation. I am talking about a situation when you may be feeling exhausted, working too hard by day, and not sleeping at night. You might feel sick often or be struggling to concentrate. Too many days of long work hours, skipping lunch, and not eating properly will eventually catch up with you. It is impossible for anyone to manage huge workloads without any break. Something has to give.

You might notice a lack of motivation, lack of interest, or alienation from others. You might feel that you have lost your grip, or be feeling less competent with tasks that you used to do easily. You might notice your productivity has waned, or that you totally lack any sense of achievement or satisfaction in your work, even though the evidence to the contrary may be in front of you. These are all characteristics of burnout. If this is you, take time off work, take time out. Reconnect with yourself, take time for exercise, eat well, socialise, and regain your sense of self that exists outside of work. Burnout is serious. Do not ignore the signs.

Shake up your routine, plan a holiday, declutter your life, and look for simplicity. Reassess your priorities and your expectations. Start by making small improvements wherever you can. Find some peace and quiet amidst your busy life. Seek out friends who will remind you that you have a sense of humour. Rather than sweat the small stuff, think big picture. Walk, drink water, and take time for relaxation. Enjoy baths, showers, swimming, or other engagement with the elements. Develop a new work philosophy so that when you return to work, you will leave your work at the office and keep time for your real life. Realign your priorities and engage with new people in your life. Take time for some travel and either act on or distance yourself from the things that stress you.

3.6. Overcoming stress, overthinking, and anxiety

Stress is a driving force—it helps you to get things done on time, to learn your lines for a play or the rules of the road if you want to get your driver's license. Stress is a huge friend—it is only a problem when you feel overwhelmed by all you have to do or when you find yourself in situations that are dampening your spirits. A busy lifestyle with lots of activities and things to remember is both exhilarating and stressful. To sit at home with nothing to do would be less stressful but possibly boring. You have to find your own healthy balance.

Understand that it is normal to have anxious thoughts. What you do with them is what determines whether or not you will end up in a state of anxiety. Everyone has anxious thoughts at different times in their lives, like the first day in a new education setting, a new job, attending a social gathering with a new group of people, travelling overseas, or even walking out the front door. Remember, anxious thoughts are what keep you safe. They stop you from walking straight onto a road where you might get hit by a passing vehicle. They stop you from touching a burning fire. They stop you diving into a relationship that you know will not be good for you. They stop you from being late to lodge your tax return.

You may create your own stress by creating such high expectations for yourself that you have no time to relax or 'do nothing' because you are always rushing to keep commitments. Being a perfectionist about everything is a sure road to anxiety. Taken to extreme, it is an impossible task because life gets complex. If you know you are a perfectionist, try to target your perfectionism in one or two areas of your life rather than in every area of your life. If your perfectionism is at the expense of life balance then sickness, or some sort of crisis, is likely to occur. If you are determined to remain a perfectionist then challenge yourself to be a perfectionist in keeping your life in balance.

3. Nurturing yourself

What is stressful for one person can be exhilarating for another. There are many ways you might stress yourself. You might anticipate all the things that could go wrong, or expect that someone won't like you. You might create stress through holding on to bad memories or old hurts instead of letting them go. You might allow your brain to focus on what-ifs rather than be in the moment. Worrying about your health is another way to whip yourself into an anxiety state. These are just examples of the kinds of thought patterns that are likely to cause you to overthink everything.

One young client was convinced he had heart problems because he could hear his heart making sounds. All medical tests revealed that he had a healthy heart, however, he was so anxious he kept researching heart problems and convinced himself his heart was faulty. When he was busy doing something enjoyable he forgot to listen to his heart. At these times he felt good and his heart was not a problem. The moment he was alone, he would start to think about it, dwell on it and convince himself there was a problem.

If you are worrying about your health, do a quick check to see if you are in serious pain, or have a high temperature. Talk to someone close if you are unsure if you need to get to the doctor. Sometimes a physical problem is a physical problem. If you think that worrying about your health is caused by overthinking and anxiety, breathe in and out slowly. Engage your brain in an activity you enjoy and see how you feel. Does it go away? If so, then it is time to take charge of your anxious thinking.

If the stress you are experiencing is severe and ongoing, then have a think about what it is that is driving your stress. Is it a need to be the best, to be approved of, or to win? Is it a fear of failure, a fear of losing the respect of others, being over critical of others or yourself? If the stress is uncomfortable then you may need to question the nature of the drive that is pushing you so hard. The stress you are putting on yourself may help you to be a high achiever, but in the long run it will do you emotional or physical damage. Envisage a life where you have fun, a life where you enjoy challenges but are not consumed by them, a life in which you are constantly enriched by the balance of your activities and enthusiastic about future challenges. This is the opposite scenario to burnout.

It is important to find something to do in your life that you enjoy and do not find stressful. This may be lazing with a good book, watching TV, or having fun with computer games. It is also good to have a safe zone or safe place where you can retreat whenever things are rough. Your bedroom may be a safe place where you feel at peace, or perhaps you have a favourite tree to sit under, or a special stuffed toy to curl up with. Even a special symbol or picture can be a safe space – it can be anything that reminds you in your heart of hearts that you are loved, that you are okay, and that you can get through anything!

Look at your time management and develop some habits that make life easier. Purchase some cheap baskets or trays to help get yourself organised. Have a bag for each activity that you restock ready for the week. Get work done according to your schedule, assess your sleep habits, and look at how much time you spend on those comfort activities. Read, relax, and try some gentle diaphragmatic breathing.

If you find the days stressful, make sure you are well-organised. Take care of the little things, like having a bottle of water ready in your gym bag, or sitting your music with your instrument, or putting your hiking gear all in the one spot, your life will be easier to manage. You will be able to give 100% to whatever activity you are involved in. When you have work to do, always start the hard tasks first and work through them one step at a time. The later ones will seem easy to finish. When you have completed each task, take a little time to celebrate your success before you move to the next task.

If your sleep routine is not good, make sure you have wind-down time without media devices before you sleep. If you find you can't relax, put your head in a happy place. Imagine a picture of your favourite or happiest place, and put your head into it as if it is a jigsaw puzzle. Think about all the individual bits that go together. Examine each part of the picture in detail.

Gradually bring forward the time for bed, but get up at the same time each day. If your sleep regime is totally out of whack and you are sleeping in late, then you will need to gradually force yourself to get up a little earlier each day until you get back to a reasonable schedule. Do it gradually, but be persistent.

Sometimes life conspires to bring lots of difficult things all at once. During these times, it is important to live one day at a time and try not to worry too much into the future. There is no point in worrying about things that may never happen. Use some relaxation exercises to calm your body and your mind. Reassure yourself that difficult things are always more manageable after a good night's sleep.

If something is worrying you, do something about it earlier rather than later. Don't let little things turn into big things because you have left it so long to take action. Allow yourself time to daydream about the things you would like to do in the future. Give space to your daydreams, but don't churn and overthink them.

Overthinking: You are more than your brain!
From the time you were little you were probably told to use your brain, to think about everything – to be sensible, to work it out, to think about consequences, to problem-solve, and to learn. You can be forgiven for thinking that you are your brain, though this is not true. The cognitive part of your brain is great for problem-solving as needed, but quite inept when it comes to emotional issues.

Emotion also comes from the brain, but for the purposes of this discussion I have chosen to regard them as coming from your heart. While emotion evolves from a number of areas of the brain, the exact nature of these connections are not yet fully understood. When the heart is examined under MRI, warm, heartfelt feelings light up the nerve endings around the heart. For therapeutic purposes, the distinction between head and heart is helpful.

The cognitive part of your brain takes in and manipulates sensory data (sight, sound, touch, taste, and smell), making neural connections (pathways) that develop into your thought patterns. The part of your brain that gives you grief with overthinking is a huge network of everything you see, hear, touch, taste, or smell. From the time you are born, the neural connections are made between all your sense data. They are stored for future reference.

Your brain is a great little computer to carry around on your shoulders, however, living in your brain will inevitably lead to stress and anxiety. It will overwhelm you because the number of neural connections in your brain are infinite. There are endless neural pathways that you can travel along in your thoughts and they interconnect with other ones. When you overthink, you ruminate, following similar neural pathways, circling them over and over. When solutions are not obvious, there can be an endless inspection of detail. The lack of a solution to an insoluble situation or a situation that is beyond your control causes distress and leads to a state of anxiety. It will leave you feeling like there is no way out.

The cognitive part of your brain takes in sense data and organises it into logical, rational ways. When you stay in your brain and see everything in a rational way, the lack of emotional and spiritual connection erodes your wellbeing. Often you can't get the green light because there is conflict with what you are feeling. When you allow yourself to drop into your emotional self, the future pathway often becomes crystal clear. You suddenly realise what it is you want. It is like making a list of pros and cons but then deciding a different pathway because you realise what you want.

If you want to become a master at managing your anxiety there are a few things you need to understand.

It is important you understand how your brain works
As the blood flows into the brain it causes the neurons to fire whenever a new connection is made. Millions of connections

3. Nurturing yourself

are formed. Some connections become automatic, like learning to walk, or starting a car. Your first efforts are pretty wobbly, but the skill gradually becomes automatic. A huge number of our behaviours are automatic. With automatic/addictive behaviours like cigarette smoking, the neural pathway is thick and strong. It is so easy to slip down the neural pathway. And yet, for each time you say no to a cigarette, you build a new neural connection that develops into a neural pathway that gets stronger and stronger until, eventually, the old cigarette pathway is pruned away through lack of use.

When you are in fight, flight, or freeze mode, two little lobes in the back of the brain called the amygdala grab the blood as it comes through the brain. In extreme fear, people do silly things because the outer part of the brain where our decisions are made does not getting sufficient blood flow with the necessary oxygen. Learning how to calm your fear and focus your brain on non-anxious thoughts is important. If you allow yourself to be consumed by anxious thoughts of failing before an exam, your capacity for thought will be reduced. Anxiety up = brain power down!

Understand that your brain never stops. That is normal. The computer was first modelled from the brain and, like the internet, there are infinite connections that can be made in the cognitive part of our brain. Thousands of thoughts are created as new neural connections are made. The neurons fire and the idea passes on to be replaced by another in rapid succession. Have you ever had the experience of having a fantastic idea only to find a second later that it has disappeared? It can be so frustrating when you just can't recall it, but the neurons have fired and the thought is gone in a flash!

Just imagine how good it would be if you allowed your anxious thoughts also to pass through your brain in a flash. This will happen once you accept that it is normal to have anxious thoughts and choose to pay no attention to them.

Anxiety happens when you insist on holding onto the anxious thoughts and then exaggerate them. 'Oh no', 'What if ...?' or,

'That is awful', and, 'If I am thinking that it must be real'. When you engage in this kind of catastrophising, anxiety is inevitable. Be aware of what the cognitive part of your head is doing. Let the anxious thoughts go and take control of what your brain is engaged in.

Find a good distraction from overthinking
Tell your brain to do something that is pleasant, fun, or productive. Refuse to engage in anxious overthinking. Sing a song, recite the alphabet backwards, construct a shopping list, or meditate. Find something that works for you. Whenever you start feeling anxious, ask your brain to engage in your favourite distraction and notice how the anxiety lifts in the short-term. You can't get anxious if your brain is working on something else. If you are too engulfed in your thoughts to do anything, look around you and use your five senses to bring you into the here and now. Everything you see, hear, smell, taste, or touch is in the present. The here and now brings relief from anxious thoughts that reside in the past or the future.

Adopt a new philosophy, rather than being ruled by anxious thoughts
Managing anxious thinking requires a shift from your head to your heart. If you struggle with identifying your feelings, it is worth taking time to try to master this shift from head to heart.

Try to come up with the vision of something that really touches your heart, like the person you love the most. When you access that emotion, note how warm and lovely the feeling is. Have your own special happy place. Hold onto that feeling. Savour and enjoy all the feelings that come to the fore. Even if it is too hard to put words to the feelings, note how strong and real those feelings can be. Get used to the idea that your heart space is a warm, comforting place. It is not somewhere you have to run away from. Your emotions are where you find your true directions in life. This is the part of you that helps you choose what you want.

3. Nurturing yourself

The power to overcome anxious thinking lies first in being aware of what your brain is doing. Then it is your strength of wanting to be or to do something in a different way that will give you the power to overcome those anxious thoughts. Once you know what you want or how you want to be, it is easy to focus your head in that direction. Think of the athletes going to the Olympics. Their extensive daily training is over four years for what is sometimes a few minutes in competition. As they get closer their thoughts are flooded with all the things that could go wrong, yet their strength lies in saying, 'Shut up, brain. I'm not going there. I WANT to focus on my training, going to the Olympics, having a great time. I want to do the best I can'. Sporting teams pay huge amounts to hypnotherapists to help motivate athletes with this kind of focus.

The neural connections in your brain are logical and rational. The brain thrives on instructions. If you tell your brain you need to get home it will dutifully tell you which way to turn until you get home. If you tell your brain to focus on, 'What if I fail', or, 'What if no one likes me', or, 'I am hopeless', it will go down that pathway and keep going with more and more what ifs until you say, 'That is enough ... I need to stop thinking that way'. If you fail to take charge of your brain you are likely to end up at the end of one of these long corridors of fearful thinking where you become depressed or highly anxious. Just like a computer, the cognitive part of your brain will dutifully carry out whatever task you give it.

Remember, you are much more than the cognitive part of your brain. You have an emotional self, a physical self, and a spiritual self. When your head, heart, and body are all working together in the moment, you are in a good spiritual space, the healthiest mental space you can ever be. Some people get this from prayer, some from sailing, or being in the forest. Sporting stars refer to this when they say, 'I was just in my zone'. This zone is in the here and now, in the moment.

Find your special spiritual place and notice how you are anxiety-free while there. When anxious thoughts intrude you have the power to choose whether you allow them to take control of you or, whether you make your brain focus in a preferred direction, one that is positive and anxiety-free.

Avert panic attacks with deep breathing and refocusing

Allowing yourself to be swallowed up in a reaction of fear will stop you from thinking through your situation in a calm and rational way. When you get anxious you hold yourself and breathe in a shallow fashion. Your brain goes into panic mode because it starts to lack oxygen. It sends a message to your heart telling it to pump harder. You heart starts pounding in your chest and you start to perspire as if you have just gone for a long run. This is an uncomfortable feeling that that can set up even more fearful thinking that the discomfort might never stop. A feedback loop develops, and you experience a full-blown panic attack.

If you become aware that a panic attack is on the way, just take in a few really big, deep breaths and the biological symptoms of a panic attack will start to wane. Open up your chest and breathe really deeply. Go outside, look around you. Ground yourself in your senses: what can you see, what can you hear, what textures can you feel around you, what can you taste, or smell? As you bring yourself into the here and now you will calm yourself.

While this gives temporary relief, the next step requires that you manage the thinking going on in the cognitive part of your brain. Make your brain focus on something of your choice, something other than the major stressor. Take time out to enjoy whatever it is that helps you feel calm.

When you later start to consider the nature of the life situation that took you into panic, you will have some decisions to make about what it is you need to change to avoid another panic situation. Calm yourself and reassure yourself that you could face even the worst case scenario. Then try to take a more balanced approach to the situation and be strict with yourself

3. Nurturing yourself

about the issues you have been catastrophising in your head. Work out your highest priority and choose how you want to handle yourself in the future.

Make the switch from your head to your heart

It is rubbish to believe that you are 'just an anxious person'; that you inherited it from a parent and are stuck with it for life. What you may have inherited is a way of dealing with the world. If you suffer from anxious thinking, then you have acquired a neural patterning that possibly destroys or demeans your self-esteem, or one that engulfs you in fear. When the anxiety takes hold, you are in fantasy of the past or the future, rather than in the present. What you have probably inherited is a tendency to believe in your head as your authority, your ruler. If there is a problem in your life, you probably believe that rational problem solving is the only way to deal with the situation.

By contrast, it is your heartfelt feelings that will often help you choose the direction in which you want your cognitive brain to focus. Once you work out what you want, you have the power to push through any anxious thought that gets in your way.

Work at distinguishing between thought and feeling on a daily basis. Ask yourself six times a day:

> *'What has been going on in my head?'*
>
> *'What am I feeling?'*
>
> *'What is my body telling me?'*
>
> *'Am I in a good spiritual space meaning my head, heart and body are all engaged in something I love?'*

If the answer is no, then set about getting yourself back into the here and now. Ask yourself what you want and how you want to be in whatever situation that is troubling you.

Remember, your thoughts are always fleeting unless you hang onto them, catastrophise them, and bring them into your reality. Just because you have an anxious thought doesn't mean that you have to listen to it. That thought is just the result of a neural connection that you have made through habit. You can't remember every single thought you had in the last 10 minutes because they pass through so quickly. The neurons have fired and ceased. Let the troublesome ones go and create some better ones. Switch from your head to your heart and ask yourself, 'What do I want? How do I want to deal with this?'

Trust your heart to overrule your head. You can then use your head just like a computer to double check the safety of your chosen journey. It can be a tool that you can use as required rather than one that dominates your whole world.

Understand that hearing voices can reflect heightened anxiety

Anxiety and stress are a big part of life – it can be what causes us to get up in the morning, to catch the bus on time, to get assignments in by the due date. If you learn to use stress to fire you up and get you into action, then you won't be caught up in overthinking everything. If you overanalyse and overthink everything you will likely end up feeling anxious, tired, and unmotivated. This is not nice!

It is not unusual to worry about your own mental and emotional health during stressful times. So often people will become anxious about being anxious. It is common to feel scared by the intensity of feelings, and it is important to understand that heightened anxiety can induce you to hear voices. I have come across young people who feel too ashamed to tell anyone because they fear they are going crazy. Hearing a voice or voices can seem convincingly real, and it can be very scary. More often than not, it is not anything psychotic, but rather a result of heightened anxiety. It is also well-known that some drugs can induce frightening visual pictures in your brain.

This feels different to self-talk which some people are not aware they use. When you are really stressed you can have a heightened awareness of your internal dialogue – you become more focused on it. Self-talk is healthy and very helpful in many situations. Athletes use it to push themselves to higher performance. Try to pay attention to your own self-talk and notice when you use it. Have a short encouraging phrase that is meaningful to you. Say it to yourself over and over again in really tough situations when you need to keep your cool and reduce your anxiety.

It is important to find out what it is that is causing your symptoms. If the voices are prompted by anxious thinking, it is easy to get help. There are anxiety management strategies that you can implement so that your anxiety never reaches those heights again. Be brave! Counsellors and medical practitioners deal with this kind of thing every day. If the symptoms seem more than an anxious focus on your self-talk, or seem to include scary visual components, then seek help, the earlier the better. Early intervention usually brings a quicker recovery. Most of the population suffer from anxiety at some time in their lives, and your symptoms need to be talked about with a doctor and/or mental health professional as soon as possible!

3.7. Dealing with depression

Depression is often the result of normal, intelligent, and sensitive responses to a world that hurts. Anyone, regardless of their age or experience in dealing with tough situations, can suffer from depression. Highly-competent people often believe they can ignore or push aside any hurt they experience in order to maintain privacy and continue their busy life. The trouble is, when the hurt is major, this process is not sustainable over the long-term.

Clients often fail to comprehend why they are feeling so depressed. They are unable to remember all the things that have led to the way they are feeling. They just complain about feeling numb and lifeless. Clients often say they feel silly because there is no one thing that they are sufficiently unhappy about to cause the way they feel. If you find yourself in this situation, know that working with a therapist will help identify all the feelings that have gone underground and the things you need to change in your life to regain your happiness. More often than not, it can be as simple as learning how to be more assertive and to reach out for the things you need.

When something goes wrong, some people tend to turn aggression inwards with destructive self-talk, while others are prone to external blaming. Neither is helpful, especially if it results in depression. If you are a self-blamer, work to push back what you don't need to take responsibility for. If you tend to blame others, identify and take responsibility for whatever you need to take responsibility for, then try to fix up any wrong you may have done.

In counselling, the therapeutic task is to integrate all aspects of yourself that have been fragmented. These sessions can be fun and productive, and should not be feared. Talking with a counsellor is different to chatting with a friend. A professional counsellor is independent from your life and is able to be objective about you and your issues. As a client it is quite a luxury to sit with someone and not have to pay any regard to them as a person. Both you and the counsellor will be free to focus totally on you. By dealing with those hurts as they gradually emerge, most clients respond well to therapy.

There are a number of unhelpful patterns of behaviour that contribute to depression: disconnection, substance abuse, hearing voices, and a belief that life should be sweet all the time. There are two entrenched patterns of thinking and feeling with which clients commonly lock themselves into depression, anxiety, and ongoing mental illness. These are negative thinking, and victim status. No amount of therapy will change these patterns unless the client is committed to changing them. These will be dealt with first.

Negative thinking
I saw a young client with suicidal ideation after reading a story about a suicide pact. The story told of a young girl who chose suicide instead of spilling her emotional secrets. My young client (herself in pain) identified with and absorbed the pain of

3. Nurturing yourself

the girl in the book. Like the girl in the book, she was worried about the pain she would cause her boyfriend if she broke up with him, and was worried about the pain she would cause her parents by not living up to their expectations of university entrance. In her blind spot was the effect her death would have on those who loved her. She had become so self-absorbed in her own perspective of her world that she became numb and disconnected from others, as well as herself. Underlying her overwhelming sadness was total negativity about the world, and about her future.

It is so easy to get trapped in the corridor of your own negative thinking. You might be trained academically to be critical and analytical. This may be quite valuable for various professional tasks. In your emotional life there is always a choice to view your situation in a positive way rather than with a negative spin. Focusing on the worst part of any situation only makes it worse. It narrows your lens to the rest of life, and for what purpose?

Some use negative thinking as a cop-out, giving themselves an excuse for not trying. They cut their life experience down at the roots. Numerous times I have heard young males, usually around the age of 16 or 17, admit that they always choose to think the worst so they never have to feel disappointed. Disappointment is just another of the myriad of emotions we feel as we go through life. Think about how much of life you are cutting yourself off from, simply by being pessimistic. Think about the opportunities for excitement that you are denying yourself.

Have the courage and humility to pull yourself up if you hear negativity in your attitude. Rather than be in the habit of breaking down, destroying or belittling your future opportunities, challenge yourself to think of positive possibilities and outcomes. It is, of course, totally your choice. You can choose to live a life of misery or you can choose to live for the great things that might happen.

Victim beliefs

If you believe that your life is controlled by external forces then you will likely find yourself thinking:

'I'm powerless.'

'My life sucks.'

'I can't change my life!'

'Who cares?'

'It is all their fault.'

Your emotional pain will be proof to you that the world is against you. If you have victim beliefs you are unlikely to seek counselling support because you don't believe anything will change. Victim approaches to living often work. There are always people who will rush to feel sorry for you, to step in and help, even to take control. This kind of behaviour meets their needs to be useful and helpful to others. It gives them a sense of worth. In this way, victim thinking can be self-perpetuating. As others do for you, you feel the need to do less for yourself, and you really do feel sorry for yourself.

The trouble is, anyone who gets really close to you will probably begin to distance themselves from you because it is too much hard work bolstering you up and trying to motivate you to do for yourself. I read somewhere that insecurity is toxic. If your respond to the world from a position of extreme insecurity, you make it very difficult for others who find themselves in a no win situation. They move away from you emotionally because no matter what they do they are unable to please you. There are similarities with victim thinking. If this is you, be bold and be honest about the way you try to manipulate others by playing the insecure victim.

Victim thinking is a state of mind that sometimes eludes individuals. Take stock of your own attitudes and your tendency to blame others. By taking on victim status you are refusing to take responsibility for your own future, and therefore get to opt out of what are often hard solutions. Rather than merely blame others, or yourself, it is important to take responsibility and take action to help yourself. Again, it is your choice. If you have this kind of belief system, you are quite free to hold onto it for the rest of your life if that is what you really want. This is something you have to sort out within yourself. In my observation, those who luxuriate in victim beliefs seem to remain continuously miserable. Nothing is ever right for them.

Disconnection

If you sense peer rejection, bullying, or suffer from anxiety and insecurity, you may experience a feeling of disconnection. When there is something major interfering with your happiness, it is too easy to slip back into an old habit of victim thinking. The trouble is the repercussions of these behaviours can bring feelings of low self-esteem and worthlessness, and you may feel like withdrawing. This is where people disconnect from those around them. If you feel like this, rather than disconnect, seek help to resolve the situation. There is always a healthier perspective that you can adopt on what is happening in your life but sometimes assistance is needed to bring those perspectives to the fore. Sometimes support is needed to take action that stops others from hurting you. If you push others away when you feel disconnected it becomes a self-fulfilling prophesy that no one cares. This is never the case. You have to let people in.

Substance abuse

Negative thinking, victim beliefs, and disconnection can easily lead people to substance abuse. It is too easy to get sucked into a short-term solution for a problem that feels too big to manage. Young clients will often tell me that their drug use started as a wonderful relief from anxiety. The trouble is, a pattern of partying and associated substance abuse might lead you to cyclical mood changes, temporary highs and subsequent lows, depression, dependence, and shame.

Substances that can cause psychotic events can change your life forever. I have seen far too many clients who date the onset of their mental illness back to psychotic events during substance abuse in their younger days. Be wise about what you are doing to yourself in difficult times. It is a time for self-nurture, not self-destruction. If you are inclined to self-sabotage, you may well end up in a far worse situation than the one you are trying to escape from.

As mentioned earlier, self-talk is useful because it distracts the brain from otherwise negative or self-defeating thoughts. Use your self-talk to help focus on what you want to do. Use self-talk when you are having a crisis of confidence. Use it to push anxious thoughts away, to help you take control, and to believe in yourself. Give your brain something to focus on instead of victim or negative thoughts. This is so much more powerful than substance abuse that may make you feel good in the short-term, but will create more problems for you in the long-term.

The belief that life should be sweet all the time
As a young adult you will be relatively new to adult understandings of the world, and possibly have little experience of life's ups and downs. You may have had a pretty smooth life with a supportive family, and be unaware that others have had a much rougher ride than you. As you enter adult life, you become more aware of world disasters and sad occurrences in the lives of your friends. Everyone has their own journey. Bad things do happen in life, but so do wonderful things. Both positive and negative emotion are part of living. It means you are alive and are experiencing the full range of life. Even with negative experiences you have the opportunity to turn that experience into something positive. Misfortune has created wonderful opportunities for people that they would never have seen otherwise.

If you unwittingly hold a belief that life should be sweet all the time, the slightest hurdle on your path is likely to stop you. When you drop your bundle and give up, you lack resilience and miss an opportunity to learn something or to reshape your future. If you hide from the world in your room, you miss out on living. Living is about experiencing great joy and great sadness, and everything in between. If something goes wrong in your own life and you are not feeling very resilient, it is important to take stock of the positives and remind yourself that you are not the first person to have this happen to you. Note that your forebears probably went through things that were much harder than what you are going through.

However bad your situation is at the moment, pick yourself up and look forward to experiences that will bring you joy. Be resilient, rather than precious. Whatever it is, you will find your way through it if you remain positive. If you resort to negativity and victim responses your life will probably get much worse. Those close to you will withdraw and you will have less support to achieve what it is you want to achieve.

Look beyond yourself. Focus on making someone else happy. Connect with someone you love. Take time out to be alone to think through your options. Rather than feed sad stories to yourself, dream some positive stories for the future. Enjoy the beauty of nature. Consider your ultimate purpose and seek out humour wherever you can. Express gratitude for what you have rather than focus on what you don't have. Make room for your dreams and conquer your worst fears.

3.8. Coping with loss

Most adults have some experience of loss. They come to understand that there is a movement through grief that takes you to a place of reconciliation, where the pain of loss is lessened as it gives way to an acceptance of a loved one being at peace. Family members may grieve in different ways and stages, and respect has to be shown to those who express their pain in different ways. When you have previously experienced grief there is some predictability about the process of grieving, and you know that you will eventually feel better.

When loss occurs, those affected need to be in the presence of their family who provide a sense of security, peace, and a perspective that life still goes on. Safety and security are key emotions that provide an environment for those healing from what is often quite a traumatic experience. In various social groups there can be unusual background beliefs that come to the fore in times of grief.

Fantasies about death
Like a television version of the real thing, vulnerable adolescents can fantasise about joining or being with the deceased. They glorify the death and the person, refusing to acknowledge that their friend had both failings and strengths. Their imaginings omit reality about the finality of death. As they themselves expect to be forever connected to their friend through grief, they think their own death will lead to some kind of eternal connection with the deceased.

Fear that pain won't go away
People with little experience of grief can find their intense feelings quite frightening. This is frequently the case with young people. They have no prior experience of moving through grief, and don't expect to ever feel normal again. To them it feels like a permanent state. Young people need to be reassured that they will eventually come to terms with what has happened and will be able to think of all the celebrated aspects of their lost one. They need to be reassured that they will eventually go back to feeling more like their old self.

When someone threatens to take their life
When someone takes their own life, the shock of what has happened torments those left behind. The aftermath is insidious and cruel. From one perspective, it is incredulous that someone would rather take their own life than put themselves through some of the inevitable pain that accompanies a journey through life. From an opposing perspective, there is tremendous compassion for anyone to be in such a numb or depressed state that they are unable to consider the impact on those left behind. It is so hard to manage these kinds of

opposite and conflicting emotions. It is confusing. How can you feel both compassion and anger at the same time? This kind of emotional confusion is draining as you bounce from one feeling to the other. Along with this kind of confusion there is often no end to feelings of frustration because there is rarely an answer to the question, 'Why?'

I see clients of all ages who live in fear because their friend or family member has threatened to take their own life. This fear produces an ongoing state of anxiety, a mixture of feeling powerless and frustrated. I also hear clients say that they fear that they will, in some way, contribute to a person's death. I often hear things like, 'I can't break up with my boyfriend because he might do something awful'; 'I can't leave my wife, she has always said she would kill herself'.

It is really hard not to get sucked into this kind of ultimate emotional manipulation. You can care for, and be there for someone, but you can't change the world for them, and you can't be there to monitor them 24-hours a day. If you are seriously concerned you should involve the mental health authorities through their crisis line. When anyone expresses suicidal intention, they lose all rights to confidentiality because they are beyond helping themselves. The person you worry about has choices. They can choose to take responsibility for themselves by reaching out to an appropriate person for help. If they refuse to do this, it is worth examining the evidence to identify whether or not this person is in the habit of taking responsibility for themselves or whether they are a frequent blamer of others.

Either way, if they prefer to depend on you, then you have to be strong enough to explain that this is too much for you. The, 'Please don't tell anyone' phrase holds no strength when someone is contemplating the taking of their own life. You have to put their welfare ahead of any fears of losing the friendship. No-one knows what life will provide around the next corner. A permanent solution to one of life's temporary situations needs to be prevented and you have to get professional help for this person as soon as possible.

This prompts an age-old question I keep asking: how is it that many people make a good recovery from mental illness, while many do not? What is it that makes someone 'turn the key' or 'flip the switch' and decide to get better? If we really understood the nature of resilience we could encourage others to heal. What is it that gives people faith in their ability to get through difficult times, to be resilient and positive at those times when life is unbearably tough?

Strategies to help in times of grief

People experience grief in many different ways. There is no right way to grieve and yet there are some indications of risk for ongoing mental health issues and self-harm. Your understanding of grief and the social custom you have grown up with will influence the way you grieve.

When you suffer a loss it is important to stay close to your loved ones rather than draw away from them. Understand that people grieve in their own way and it is important to be tolerant of others. One member of the family might seem to be fully over the loss because they are not at all teary, whereas another is unable to stop the tears. Tensions can be high when family members make judgments of other family members, saying that they act like they don't care. It is a different journey for everyone and what appears on the surface is not necessarily the same as what is experienced deeply. It is a time to refrain from judgement and a time to be patient and tolerant of others.

When someone dies, there is usually something left undone or unsaid. Death never happens conveniently, and you need to be very gentle with the way you treat yourself. Guilt is not helpful. Neither is the reaction of wanting to blame someone. It is an understandable reaction, but you need to stop yourself from thinking that way.

If someone close to you has taken their life, understand that it is a very natural response to feel guilt for not having been able to prevent the tragedy. There is always something you wish you could have done or said. Try to respect the person's choice even

3. Nurturing yourself

if you disagree with it. There is no more deliberate act than to take one's own life. You cannot make a person walk from Point A to Point B unless they wish to do so. The deceased made their choice, and they chose not to reach out for help. In many cases they have worked very hard to conceal their distress and their intentions.

Those left behind often chastise themselves for not seeing the signs of distress that led to this very sad choice. It is important to remember that the best experts are unable to accurately determine which individuals will action suicidal thoughts. I also know that many individuals who take their lives are often extremely crafty about not letting anyone know their pain or their plans. When they do tell someone, it is curious that they often choose to tell someone they know who will brush them off. Self-blame is not helpful. This was not your choice.

Know that once you allow yourself to express your grief, you will move through it to another set of feelings. Feelings are temporary. No matter how bad you feel, you will find that you will move to a different emotional place.

Whatever your loss, take time out to grieve in the way that feels right for you. Try not to stop yourself from shedding tears. Give yourself time to grieve. When you feel ready to resume your daily duties, make sure others around you know that you may need some time out every now and again. You might feel you can't let the loved one leave your thoughts, or that you need to stay true to them by continuing to think about them all day, every day. This is not what your loved one would want. Try to push yourself through during the day, and allow yourself a dedicated time at the end of the day when you can allow yourself to grieve freely. It might help to use this time to remember or write down your reflections. It might help to use this time to find a special place where you can converse with your lost one in your head. Try to express the things that you feel you left unsaid. Find a special way to celebrate or commemorate your loved one.

4

Getting serious about relationships

- *4.1. What makes a relationship healthy?*
- *4.2. Contributing strength to your relationship*
- *4.3. How do you know when you have met the right partner?*
- *4.4. No matter what you do, it is just not working*

4.1. What makes a relationship healthy?

If your relationship is healthy, there is a fluidity that allows each partner to grow and change. It will be easy to move in and out of the intimate emotional connection. Each of you will be engaging in different outside worlds that challenge, invigorate, stress, or maybe even disappoint. The intimate connection provides balance, stability, and security through an understanding that your partner will respect, support, and show a caring for you when things don't go so well. Your partner will also enjoy the fun times with you. When you have a lifetime partner you will have a sense of ongoing friendship and commitment, with a myriad of understandings that you co-create.

Entering an intimate relationship can require a degree of personal courage. Trusting your emotional wellbeing to the hands of another is like abseiling, like putting your life-blood in the hands of a surgeon or a pilot, where you know the outcome will be either life-enhancing or life-diminishing, depending on their skill. We trust implicitly that our surgeons and pilots are motivated to do their best for us. This is not the same in a relationship. When we start a new relationship, we can never be sure that our trust will be well-founded. It takes time to know how much you can trust another. All you can do is work on making yourself into a whole human being who is able to withstand the difficult aspects of relationships.

To be a whole human being you must be able to know what you are thinking, to be able to identify what you are feeling, to understand what your body is telling you, and to have some sense of your spiritual awareness. To be whole, you need to be able to draw on and integrate these aspects of yourself. It is fruitless to debate feelings at a cognitive level because feelings are not necessarily logical or rational. While ideas may be debated back and forth forever, feelings cannot be debated; they just are. Feelings need to be acknowledged, held, and responded to in a respectful manner. Where thoughts can be disputed, feelings should never be discounted.

In a healthy relationship your partner will 'hold' your emotion, i.e. hear and empathise, without rushing in to fix the problem. While problem solving skills are useful for sorting the many differences that may arise in your relationship, they often get in the way of empathic connection. If your partner is distressed, take time to sit with them. Show you care by listening and comforting him or her. I like the idea of the holding tank that you place metaphorically in front of you. Let the emotion flow in there. Just let it happen. If you jump in with 'fix-it' solutions, you deny your partner the feeling that you care. You stop them expressing themselves. Your partner will, in time, move through the distress. When this happens there is a very important question to be asked: 'What would you like me to do to help?' or 'What can I do to help you feel a little better?'

Some people seem to have been programmed to be the problem-solver. They tell me they find it so hard to sit back and not get into logical and rational argument about why their partner should not be so distressed. They miss the point! This is about your partner's need to communicate his or her distress. In a healthy relationship partners feel free to be themselves and are confident that their partner will support them in every way possible. The partners will work together as a team rather than one depending on the other.

Appreciating and thriving on difference

After the tumult of the first attraction subsides, differences can emerge that prove irritating. Is this just a little hiccup in getting to know someone, something that can be sorted out, or is it a problem area that will get bigger over time to become a real stumbling block in the relationship? The more you focus on differences, the greater and more worrisome they become.

There can be differences in ethnic, socio-economic, social, educational, philosophical, or religious backgrounds. There can be differences in style of living, initiative, dreams, recreational interests, literature or media interests, sense of colour, taste, smell, touch, or sound. There can be differences in beliefs around parenting, education, politics, libido, and finance. There can be differences in how one treats a neighbour, or differences in personal or daily habits.

Differences can be huge in number and kind. The list is endless. The more you add to the list, the more it seems a miracle when two people are able to mesh all these things in a way that results in a happy and productive life for both. When all these aspects do not easily mesh, relationships often break up. If this happens, it is important to acknowledge that the amount of difference is what prevented the relationship surviving, rather than blaming the other, or assaulting one's own self-esteem.

While difference may pull your relationship apart, difference, at the same time, is what defines you as individuals. It is difference that can either bring life and vitality to a relationship, provide inspiration, growth and adventure. So where is the happy medium? How does one choose the right partner or decide whether or not to break up a relationship that does not feel 100% right? What does it mean to have got it right, to find a relationship that will sustain itself over many years? It is certainly easy to recognise when the match turns out to be bad. These are good and sensible questions to be asking. Of course, the answers are not so easy.

It is truly inspiring to witness those relationships that weather life's storms, to witness how love can persist and sustain in the face of all sorts of personality differences and difficult circumstances. What is it about those amazing operating systems that stay robust even under extreme stress?

What I notice about long-term relationships is a deep respect and caring with a determination never to let the other down. It must surely be a good start to choose a partner you not only love, but also like and respect, one who enhances your sense of wellbeing and self-respect. While it helps if there is a strong sense of teamwork and mutual respect, it is commitment to each other that seems to stand the test of time.

Living together is easy, it seems. Young and old often jump into domesticity very quickly in the early days of relationships without much consideration of the long-term ramifications. There are couples who moved in together very early in the relationship, sign a lease only to find that one partner has extensive debt and can't afford to pay their share of the rent. On the other hand, I have seen many of these partnerships take respectful account of the other's need to pursue career goals. High-functioning and highly-intelligent young couples often negotiate shared living arrangements very well. They are savvy about buying as tenants in common, and keen to maintain their independence and their own set of friends. In theory this should work well.

The living together gives an experience of what it is like to be fully-committed on all levels of the relationship, from domestics, to holidays, and household purchases. One would think there would be little to go wrong, and yet I have seen young couples like this who enter a slump in their relationship that presents as much bigger than the usual communication issues.

4. Getting serious about relationships

The problem that emerges with these relationships is often a sense of confusion about where their life is going, and a sense of frustration with daily living. These couples seem to have missed a step in their relationship. While they never made a conscious decision to fully commit, they find themselves committed, never having given their full consent. Typically, the group of friends has narrowed, their outside interests have waned, and the relationship has becomes claustrophobic. Both find it increasingly difficult to break off the relationship because, after all, it is not 'all that bad'. On the surface, nothing is really wrong.

If you miss the step of commitment and communication about shared goals and have become comfortable in your existence together but feel totally stuck, it is time to get assistance. Only through revisiting basic values and goals can you sort out what you want. It takes brave communication to address issues that you have buried during daily transactional living. Much can be said for open discussion about commitment before you enter new living arrangements. Be clear with each other about the stage your relationship is at. Discussion needs to take place before you move in together. You need to have a thorough knowledge of anyone you share a home with. Make sure you are on the same page when it comes to finances, food and household purchasing, cleaning and tidiness habits, washing, and invited guests.

There is a common understanding that males are more likely to seek sex before intimate connection, whereas females are more likely to seek emotional connection before sex. Unless there is understanding and appreciation of the many differences between partners, these differences will provide fertile ground for conflict. What is critical is that couples communicate with each other about the multitude of small, and not so small difficulties that present in any relationship/family so that the navigations through these difficulties do not become defining events. The appreciation of difference is critical in maintaining a good relationship, however it should be remembered that each partner also contributes a unique set of skills and strengths.

4.2. Contributing strength to your relationship

Need often propels people into a relationship like a helicopter charging into a thunderstorm, determined to beat it. If you have a desperate need for intimacy, be very careful. It can drive you so hard and so quick into the 'dream' relationship that you can be blind to any negative signs that indicate future disaster. It is so easy to project on to the other what you most need to see, only to find out a month later that this new person is not who you thought they were – they do not match up to the image you projected onto them.

Accept that the yearning for a long-term partner is a normal part of human existence. The more you focus on this yearning, the less likely it is that you will find it. If you become more and more intense because you have not found a long-term partner, this will show in your demeanour and will likely work in the opposite direction. If you get on with your life and focus on making your life exciting and fulfilling, others will be attracted to your enthusiasm and your confidence.

With each new relationship you form from the day you are born you develop likes and dislikes. With each experience you gain a deepening insight into what kinds of relationships will work for you. Eventually, one day you will meet someone with whom you feel confident you can build a long and happy future. Knowing yourself well as an independent person is a necessary precursor to developing sound relationships.

You have to go into a relationship with trust that the other person will do the right thing by you. You have to give your partner the benefit of the doubt. Hopefully you will see them bring their own strength to your relationship, and they will step up to join you in a committed relationship. If you are also independent, true to yourself, and committed, you will also be contributing strength to the relationship. Remember, it takes two to make a relationship thrive.

Being independent and true to yourself
People often seek out relationships to feel complete. While this is a commonly accepted idea, there is likely to be difficulty if this

4. Getting serious about relationships

is taken to the extreme. If you are dependent on your partner for your self-esteem or self-worth, or need the presence of your partner to validate your existence, then you are on dangerous ground. A relationship solely based on need is doomed to fail.

Extreme dependence is dangerous in you or in your partner. If you need someone else, or need to be needed by someone else, it reflects a warped sense of what loving is about. Love is about caring for another, not having your own needs met. Love is about having a capacity to be loving, rather than about having a capacity to be loveable. To be loving towards another takes confidence, maturity, and a sense of being true to yourself.

If you are true to yourself you are not fabricating your personality to be what you think someone else wants you to be. You will be honest and confident in what you like and don't like but be willing to make compromises. You won't have to rely constantly on someone else to tell you how attractive you are to tell you what to do. You will have high self-esteem and will not need to play ego games or hold forth about your viewpoints in order to gain a sense of power. Having confidence in your own ability to live with ambiguity and uncertainty in the world means that you have no need to resort to black and white explanations of the world. Rather than need someone else to tell you what to think or to provide you with simple straight-forward views of life and morality, you will trust your own judgement. You will also have faith in your own ability to direct your own life, rather than be attracted to spiritual cults or religions that try to influence and control you in the guise of true belief or complete faith. Being strongly religious is not about having blind faith.

Gain your independence and learn to stand alone before you go into a serious relationship. Learn how to be your own person and to be true to yourself. When you feel independent, well-grounded, and know who you are, it will be attractive to go into a relationship based on a strong want to be with the other person, rather than needing to be with them. This is a far healthier scenario than looking for someone to complete you.

Embracing your independence
Have time on your own, live on your own, explore the world unattached, and have adventures. Exert your independence in any way that is open to you. Think for yourself rather than follow popular belief. When independence is offered to you in the form of work, take it. Don't be lazy. If you are still living in the family home then do so as an adult participant, doing your own chores and a share of the household work.

If both parties in a relationship are independent and confident in themselves there is a chance of the relationship becoming a long-term one. When tough times come, it takes two to sort out difficulties and resolve conflict. It takes courage in both partners to search out the areas that need addressing and then to resolve the communication gaps that have contributed to the problem.

Much work is done in therapy to teach people how to engage in significant connection with their partner or 'would-be' partner. Significant connection occurs only when there is a genuine interest in the other, a willingness to reach out to the other and to share one's own vulnerabilities. It is a gradual learning path that can be rocky. It involves honesty and 'learning to trust' tempered by an ability to see any red flags that indicate the other is not in the relationship for the best reasons.

Communicating well
When couples communicate in a free and easy manner, relationships tend to run smoothly. No matter how good your relationship, your communication skills will, at some time, be tested. It is inevitable that tough life situations will arise. Conflict is easily solved if both partners have the skills to communicate what they think, feel, and prefer to happen. This approach seems too simple to pay attention to. However it is one of the most common aspect of communication skills taught in therapy rooms. Without attention to the 'I' think, 'I' feel and the 'I' prefer communication is invariably loaded with 'You' judgements which increase hostility. Owning all aspects of your communication opens the way for good

connection with your partner. This model of communication allows for a full expression of each partner's thoughts, feelings and preferences. As you reach the realisation that you each of you have different preferences, what follows is a problem-solving process to work out a win-win situation so that each partner still gets their needs met. Committed couples will go to great lengths to keep their loved one happy and are therefore prepared to compromise when it is called for.

It is important to develop the courage and fortitude to look at the cracks in your relationship before they deepen and grow wider. The bigger the gap, the harder it is to close. Sometimes issues are brought into the relationship from childhood, parental influence, or from gendered expectations. Sometimes they are reflections of unconscious attitudes that just pop to the surface. More often than not, issues appear as a result of poor communication skills and situations where what is said is not what is actually meant. It takes commitment and work and sometimes a lot of tears to bridge these breakdowns in communication.

People approach conflict and emotional expression in different ways. Often one partner will feel more comfortable speaking to a stranger about relationship difficulties when they should be talking to their partner. Some couples enjoy the closeness of doing shared things with each other, then talking later, whereas others like to express their emotions before they can make an intimate connection. They like to talk over, to toss around and 'play' with their complex set of feelings until they take on form and substance. There are a multitude of ways that individuals and couples approach and deal with conflict. It is really helpful to work out the differences in the way each of you approach difficult issues. Often it is not until one partner expresses their true feelings of hurt underlying their angry outbursts that disputes begin to be resolved. If you can analyse the pattern you go through you may be able to short circuit the process to find a quicker resolution.

Your thoughts and ideas can be debated forever, whereas your feelings are personal.

Once you express a true feeling it cannot be disputed. It is a direct report of your inner experience. It may not be appropriate, acceptable, logical, just, or even balanced, yet if it is expressed honestly it is the foundation of true connection. While you can express your own reactions to what others feel, once you try to debate the validity of another's feelings you step into dangerous ground, into power and control. While it may be hard to hear someone else's true feelings they have to be respected for what they are. If you ridicule, deny, minimise, or disrespect someone's feelings they will quickly lose their respect for you. This kind of hurt is not easily erased.

In couples therapy it is magic to observe how relationships seem to become instantly unlocked when one or other partner has the courage to express their true emotion.

4.3. How do you know when you have met the right partner?

It is not surprising that you might agonise over whether your current relationship is the 'right one', the one you have been waiting for your whole life, the one you want to last a lifetime. It is a decision that young people feel compelled to make often under the strong and competing influences of close friends, family, and the ticking biological clock.

The older you get, the more you will see and understand the complexity of relationships. To bring together two people into lifetime companionship involves bringing together and meshing two different worlds. When you consider the vastly different beliefs, assumptions, expectations, values, life practices, attitudes, and habits that individuals bring to a relationship, it seems a miracle when two lives mesh so well that the couple remain happily together for a lifetime.

There seems to be a myth that there is only one right relationship. I have seen how partners bring out different personalities in each other. If you are clear in your own mind about the kind of relationship you want and how you want to be in the relationship then you will be in a better position to know when you have found a partner who will suit you. Without giving thought to this you might find yourself swept up in love with someone who is totally unsuited to you.

Potentially there may be many relationships that might be right for you, however, it takes time to really get to know someone before you have confidence in your capacity to love them for the long-term. For many people, once they love someone they don't stop loving them. Whether you will continue to like and respect your partner is another question altogether. It is like and respect that sustains relationships.

If you no longer like or respect your partner, the struggle to maintain the relationship may never erode the love you feel, but it can destroy the viability of the relationship. Being true to yourself and expressing your hopes, fears, and preferences is the only way to safeguard your future journey. Partners will change things about themselves if they truly love, care for, and respect the person making the criticism. Communication is always the key to resolving differences.

Falling in love

I once heard intimacy described as 'luscious'. It is usually a part of the phenomenon referred to as falling in love. This emotional state produces powerfully overwhelming emotions that have inspired music, film, and theatre through the ages. It is a consuming experience that renders some speechless, while others become garrulous and effusively descriptive. It can even produce physical symptoms with your heart 'jumping', or 'missing a beat'.

You may see your loved one as the answer to your dreams and hopes, or inspiring a feeling of completeness. This love may fill your thoughts day and night, creating new dreams out of vague yearnings. You might feel blessed. When the feeling is mutual, there can be an intense and extensive communication as two lives become 'synched'. You might come to know every aspect of the other's day including thoughts, feelings, secrets, and spiritual yearnings. Through this kind of communication you learn about intimacy. You learn about the requirement of trust, forgiveness, and the need for 'give and take' that keeps the relationship balanced. It is exciting to find yourself in a special twosome.

There is great joy in the sense of not feeling alone. There is a natural desire to want to grab onto this, to want more and more emotional intimacy, not to mention physical intimacy. Beware! This close and continual intertwining of experience might eventually lead to one of you feeling a little claustrophobic, enmeshed, or trapped. If this happens to you, talk it through with your partner before one of you exits from the relationship. When these feelings are brought into the open, modifications can be made, assurances given, and mutual independence created.

Over time, the experience of falling in love settles to a more steady sense of loving. Routines, expectations, and daily life find their way into the relationship. Some will report that they have stayed in love, others report a deepened love that only gets even deeper over time. In new relationships, after the first flush of falling in love, other issues can creep in. One partner might start to feel shut off from the old pre-relationship world that was once so familiar and is now missed. Another might simply miss the space to please themselves to do what they want, when they want. Sudden insights can bring fear accompanied by a fight or flight response.

These discomforts sit underneath the surface of daily living unless they are talked about. Most of these issues are normal adjustments to a change in lifestyle. Communication is what makes the difference. There is little that can't be solved if good communication takes place. Freedom and space are critical for each partner to have, and this can require regular strategic planning, especially when the family includes a busy life with children.

Unlike a state of enmeshment that demands partners do everything together, a healthy relationship allows each partner to be free to have time to continue their own personal interests outside the partnership. With competing demands of family life, this time allocation might be reduced due to circumstance, but should never be eliminated from the family's strategic plan for the year. If each of you is able to enrich your lives through your individual passions, there is a greater chance of remaining in love and deepening your love through shared experiences.

Are relationships meant to be easy?
I have often heard myself say, 'Look, if you are having this much trouble negotiating a happy pathway when your relationship is only six months old, how do you think you will cope with the next 50 years together?' If you are arguing, bickering, or misunderstanding each other's motives then it is probably time to question what it is that holds you in the relationship. Is it fear of change? Is it fear of hurting the other? Is it fear of being alone?

Of course, any healthy relationship will have testing times. There will be issues that need to be resolved, however, if the resolution is painstakingly long and arduous, there is a problem with how much emotional energy is being sapped from each of you. If you are able to resolve, forgive, forget, and move on there is hope that this will be the pattern for the following decades. If you are learning from your mistakes and the relationship is becoming easier then there is a promising pathway ahead.

I don't believe any long-term relationship is easy, but some can be much more difficult than others. When each person behaves in a mature and respectful way and there is an easy flow of energy and a compatibility in your wants and beliefs, then there is potential for easy meshing. A team of two is created. This team has the power to overcome all kinds of obstacles when there is solid commitment to teamwork.

To recap on communication:

If there is conflict over an issue and each partner is able to say what they think and feel about the issue, and what they prefer to happen, then there is a negotiation point where compromise can be reached before moving on to the next issue. There is no getting away from the fact that issues will always present in relationships. It is always healthy to have different perspectives, but it is not helpful if either of you are arrogant or belligerent in holding to your point of view at all cost. This only prevents issues from being resolved. Similarly, finger pointing and judgemental comments only serve to demean the other. Both partners need to respect difference in the other and trust that the other's motivations are well motivated.

If you can resolve conflict in a respectful and caring way and you both have trust in the other's motivations, the relationship will thrive. This is just as important as the love you feel when you start out in a new relationship.

4.4. No matter what you do, it is just not working

It is relatively easy to fall in love, and it can be very sad and confusing after loving someone deeply to then find that you intensely dislike your partner, do not want their children, or any kind of future with them. It is often called 'falling out of love'. On the other hand, you can still love someone even though you do not necessarily like them.

For a relationship to stand the test of time, love is insufficient without liking. When people come to therapy for support to break up a relationship they know in their head is over, the problem is often that their heart is still hanging on. They are in a no-win situation, wanting to love their partner and to love the image of the person they fell in love with, but at the same time having to recognise that this person is not the person they first thought them to be. Sometimes there is an ever-growing mountain of evidence that love is lacking, but it is hard to let go of the luscious, romantic feelings of intimacy experienced in the beginning. Even when there is violence or emotional abuse, there is considerable grief in letting go of the idea of being in a relationship. What has to be let go is the perceived sense of dependency on the relationship.

If cracks do appear in your relationship and you understand the dynamics of what is happening you will be well-equipped to save the relationship from larger pitfalls. Projection is one of these dynamics.

Understanding the impact of projection on new relationships

Just as an artist projects all their senses into a painting, so too do human beings cast onto the object of their desire every kind of imagining that fits with their dream. Strong need and determination to find someone who is kind and caring can lead to a projection of these qualities onto someone when in reality they may be absent. How often do you hear people say, 'I thought he was so [X] when I first met him, but now I find he is nothing like that'? All kinds of wondrous imaginings have been projected onto the 'new' love, only to find out that he or she is not at all who you first thought.

What was first experienced was largely a figment of need or desire, rather than a true appreciation of the other. You can project all the attributes you want onto another and truly believe the person is the answer to your dreams, or you can simply adopt a wait-and-see attitude that allows you to get to know the person for who they really are, not what you imagine them to be. While these projected imaginings form a natural part of attraction, it is more likely that the greater your need driving the projection, the greater the chance you will be extremely blind to the person's weaknesses. The ultimate realisation often comes when deeper belief systems are challenged, causing the relationship to break up. Typically, the person projecting the fantasies becomes quite angry when their dream is not realised. It is not nice to be on the receiving end of this.

In the early stages of an argument, partners will blatantly project elements of their own imaginings or their own past experiences on to their partner: 'She is not interested in me – only her girlfriends', or, 'He cares more about his precious football'. Judgements breed hostility, whereas owning one's own projections leaves the door open, setting the scene for discussion rather than argument. For instance, 'You are just like my mother' might be replaced with, 'I am uncomfortable when you do that because I am reminded of the way my mother used to chastise me'.

What is said in an angry moment or mumbled to someone outside the relationship can shake the foundations of a relationship. There are many ears outside the relationship that will pick up on your dissatisfaction, however, they are the wrong ears to hear your concerns. There seems to be this funny notion that if you 'put it out there' the universe will somehow convey it to the place it needs to go. When something disheartens or annoys you, rather than blab to everyone else, make sure you talk directly to your partner. Your partner is the only one who is capable of acting on what needs to be changed.

Childhood sweethearts
In your adolescence you will have noticed that relationships amongst your friends were often emotionally intense and all-consuming. When couples meet during adolescence and stay together over a long period of time they often report a deepening love as each person grows and develops a strong identity through individual achievements. Mutual respect plays a part in this deepening love. There is a commitment made to share a lifetime through a wish to be together, rather than a need fuelled by dependence or distrust.

On the other hand, romantic relationships formed during adolescence often tend to wane to reveal a relationship that is starkly inadequate for one, or both partners. The breakup is usually devastating for those involved because the relationship has lasted a whole lifetime, it seems. If this happens to you, it is important to give careful thought to the whole nature of

4. Getting serious about relationships

relationships before you go blaming yourself, or suffering a blow to your self-esteem. A breakup should never be seen as 'failing'. Do not take any notice of people who criticise you for the breakup. Anyone who judges you needs careful scrutiny for pure self-interest. Trust your own reflections on what went wrong. Take responsibility for any mistakes you have made. Be honest with yourself. Ask yourself if you would have made those mistakes if the relationship was more important to you. If this is the case, then you need to ask yourself why you are less committed than previously. Is there something you are missing in the relationship or something you are not coping with?

Acknowledgement, acceptance, and forgiveness of your mistakes gives you power to learn, move on, and do things differently. Couples often come to therapy to sort out what is going wrong. When there is open conversation and each has the capacity to reflect more on their own mistakes rather than blame the other, a deeper understanding is often reached. They will say things like, 'If only [X] had wanted children', or, 'She just needed to socialise much more than me', or, 'I was so obsessed by my sport that there was no time for us'. Ask yourself, would the breakup have occurred if there had been a better meshing of all aspects of your personalities and lifestyles? It is admirable when couples freely acknowledge that their basic differences have grown so big that they have become sticking points in the relationship.

It takes two

In relationships you cannot always be certain that the other person's convictions are honourable, or working in your favour. You trust in the hope that the other will remain committed. But there are two in the relationship, and you can only account for yourself. Relationships that feel like gold can sometimes turn to poison. They can be empowering or disempowering, fun or misery, intriguing or boring, comfortable or plain hard work, vulnerable or resilient. What is it that turns gold to poison? What is it that diminishes that which starts out so positively?

Trusting the motives behind behaviour

Good relationships are often demolished through simple mistrust of a partner's motives. There are classic stories that get told in therapy, like the flowers that get delivered with the wrong girl's name on the card, or the text message that appears out of the blue saying, 'Hi, beautiful, ring me later tonight'. So easily can a seed of mistrust be planted! So easily can paranoia set in, especially if there is a lack of openness in the relationship, or where one person is very insecure about holding onto their partner. The insecure partner drives the other partner away through total frustration with the ongoing barrage of accusation.

When let down by another's behaviour, there is temptation to respond from one's own insecurity: 'She hasn't called me … I am obviously not high on her priority list'. If you focus on the negative possibility it becomes reinforcing as behaviours are interpreted in the light of your negative expectations. It is like viewing the cup as half-full or half-empty; there is a choice. When things go wrong and bad things happen or misunderstanding occurs, it is critical to ask, 'What is this person's motive behind the behaviour? Have I got something wrong, did I misunderstand, is there something I don't know?' By all means, express what hurts, but it is also worth suspending judgement until you have a full knowledge of what went wrong.

Sometimes life conspires to create some crazy connections. With those who supposedly love you and you them, surely it is important that you give them the benefit of your doubt. This response is so much more productive than jumping to outrage and becoming entrenched in one's own position. Standing on principle only exacerbates conflict and poisons the pathway forward.

Respecting boundaries

It is always disheartening to witness a total lack of respect for another person's personal space or personal business. There is a big distinction between letting off steam or venting a little, and heartfelt emotion. If you say things in confidence to a third party who then betrays your confidence, it may do untold damage to your relationship. Even when not repeated, the information can cause subtle changes in other peoples' attitudes to your partner. Be careful who you confide in and always explain if you are just letting off steam. Acknowledge that you are only giving one side of the story. Friendships and relationships are easily destroyed. If you need to vent to your friend, you probably need to be talking to your partner instead. What is between two people needs to remain between two people. Having the wisdom to know who you can trust to hold your confidence is one of the pillars of sound friendship.

If you are on the receiving end of confidential material, repeating it to a third person may end up being highly manipulative behaviour. It is not your own information, so you have no right to pass it on. You either have to adopt a policy of remaining tight-lipped with your information about others, or be prepared to take responsibility should your words travel where they should not.

When someone declares they need space, this has to be respected. While you may think it unnecessary from your perspective, this is not the point. Respecting boundaries is about appreciating the rights of another to determine who enters their physical, mental or emotional space. If someone leaves the room to escape from a discussion they feel uncomfortable about for any reason, it is rude and disrespectful of their right to personal space to follow them. No means no in many contexts. Similarly, if you ignore someone's request for you to leave, you are being abusive. If someone says they do not wish to talk about something, it is abusive to press them to do so. It is harassment.

Maintaining your own standard of behaviour
When there is a serious impasse it is common to witness couples vehemently defend themselves. Strong ego needs often drive point-scoring behaviour. Tit-for-tat behaviour is fuelled by the need to get back at the other person. Power plays can

escalate unless at least one party has the wisdom to draw back from the fight and look at the issue to be solved, rather than the need to win the argument or attain a sense of power.

The fighting game has to stop to create a space in which to declare a time for straight and honest communication. The therapeutic setting often provides this space. It gives an opportunity for issues to be aired with support from the therapist to keep communication constructive. Acknowledging all the things that are working well helps the couple to keep a positive focus. It also helps to determine exactly how much of the relationship is causing lack of harmony. In the course of this discussion it is very sad when couples admit that they do not feel proud of the way they have been behaving. When tensions escalate and conflict persists, it is very easy to lower the standard of your own behaviour and adopt ways of relating that you would never normally stoop to. Be careful! When you cease to be reasonable or kindly to your partner, you are likely to lose your partner's respect. Respect is not easily regained.

Understanding the impact of enmeshment
In new relationships, there is often great joy in being with the loved one 24-hours a day, seven days a week. Partners are often keen to do everything together until one partner begins to feel claustrophobic and needs their own space. This sets up panic in the other. As one retreats, the other pursues and catastrophises the situation. Communication can easily break down unless there is a maturity in each partner that celebrates both independence and intimacy.

When you establish an intimate relationship with another, there is inevitably a loss of identity, especially with a first experience of enmeshment. This can be a pleasant feeling as you start to think of yourself as a couple. In a mature relationship, it is the ability to balance your need for independence with your ability to merge and draw away from your partner that determines successful intimacy.

Enmeshment is a sense that one knows the other's thoughts and feelings better than one's own. When extreme, it is common to hear phrases like, 'I feel her disappointment', or, 'I can really feel his pain'. Extreme enmeshment is commonly seen in teenage relationships, but can also be seen in couples of any age where both parties have become so dependent on each other that, individually, they have abandoned or buried their own sense of self. Empathy on the other hand, is about being able to understand another's feelings and to share them through that understanding. It is the notion of sharing rather than living the other person's feelings that makes it different. When each partner truly believes that they think and feel 'for' the other, there is such a blurring of the boundaries between 'self' and 'other' that one partner can start to feel trapped or lost. An overwhelming need to break free from the relationship often develops very suddenly. The drive to differentiate from the other looms quickly in a desperate effort to regain a sense of self that has been lost.

There are many difficulties that emerge when enmeshment is strong in a relationship. It is easy to be drawn into another's pain, the intensity in the relationship being mistaken for intimate connection. It is easy to be attracted to someone who is fragile. Their vulnerability buoys your own ego and helps you forget your own feelings of inadequacy. With shared experiences of pain there are often secrets revealed and this creates a sense of emotional intimacy. Sometimes sexual intimacy is experienced as a solution to feelings of loneliness. The effect is, of course, not long-lasting, and can lead to even deeper feelings of loneliness.

When I see a client who is 'needy' and unhappy, I often find out through discussion that they have become really enmeshed with their partner, and have lost their sense of self. Clients can be quite adamant that they feel their partner's pain. It is so easy to convince yourself that you truly know what the other is experiencing, however, you can never know someone else's experience unless they are willing to trust you enough to share it openly with you. Even then, your own pain as a listener will be different. In reality, while you may comfort the other in their pain and put yourself in their shoes to understand what they are going through, your reaction and your response is a product of our own experience and imaginings. When you are sufficiently aware of your own pain, and are able to express or offer what you feel in an appropriate way, then there is a chance that your comfort may help the other feel less alone in their pain. There needs to be a subtle balance in distinguishing *your* pain as distinct from *their* pain.

Focusing too much on yourself can take away from the experience of the other. Standing by someone in pain takes skill, sensitivity, and balance. Unfortunately, there is no way to protect, minimise, or remove pain for another human being, and we can't expect that someone else can take away our own pain.

The best you can do is to acknowledge the pain of the other and be sufficiently aware of your own feelings that you can offer them honestly, as a way of validating the other's experience. This may be in the form of tears, or words, or hugs, remembering that pain is the loneliest of all life experiences. Just being with someone in intense emotional pain provides comfort.

Enmeshment often plays a role in relationship breakups. Sometimes people come for couples counselling in order to break up a relationship that they know is already over in both their head and their heart. What they find difficulty with is breaking the enmeshment pattern that has been established, sometimes over many years. The problem is often that their heart is still hanging on. They love, and want to love the person so much that it breaks their heart to let go, even though they know they must do so. This can apply to either partner. The unclear boundaries caused by enmeshment can permeate all aspects of the breaking up process, making it a confusing time for all.

Enmeshment issues evolve gradually. Early on, there are red and green flags that may alert you about issues that will support or diminish your relationship over time.

Red and green flags in relationships

A mature-age client recently asked me what he should look for in his next relationship, since he had failed the last two miserably. I reminded him that being in a long-term relationship required a good 'match', rather than a personal failure or success. We discussed ways one could determine a benchmark below which there was a mismatch and not worth pursuing. Not an easy task given that love overcomes many negatives. It took us quite a long time to list the negative 'red flags' that he personally needed to be on the lookout for should he engage in any more relationships. While this client had learned the hard way over many years of disastrous relationships, the same list may well be relevant to young people starting out on the matching process.

Red flags – personality factors to look out for in new relationships

- A need to dominate and control
- Undue neediness and insecurity
- Addiction
- Anger/hostility towards the world in general
- Two-faced behaviour
- Financial ineptness/disregard for the need to budget
- Bullying behaviour

Green flags – personality factors that aid in sustaining relationships

- The ability to trust and be trusted, to be honest
- The ability to reflect and act on one's own faults
- Caring and considerate
- The ability to cooperate and share
- Initiative in both responsibility and fun
- A degree of intellectual ability
- Physically attractive
- Sense of fun

This mature client did not place physical attraction high on his list. It was all the other behaviours that he had found destructive in his relationships. They were the ones that he said he could not face again. Red flags will vary for each person. They can be overlooked, but only at a price that demands you accept and live with the consequences.

When I come across young ones who are intent on destroying their own self-esteem by blaming themselves for a relationship that did not survive, I feel compelled to bring what I call 'bad news'; that it is most likely that they will fall in love a number of times before they find the compelling relationship that remains comfortable and strong over a lifetime. It is actually a lucky break to find out early in a relationship that there is insufficient meshing for the relationship to work. A relationship involves two people. What is perfect for one may not be so for the other. That is 'life and love'. Treat each new relationship as a new adventure, rather than the answer to all your hopes and dreams.

Couples come to therapy often when they are at their wits' end, when their communication has become so destructive in nature that the future looks very bleak. Often there is considerable negative energy present. Facing each other in conversation, the patterns of interaction that seem to destroy the possibility of real connection become evident. The desire to regain lost intimacy is often strong, and it is curious that they find themselves so trapped in such a state of angst even though there is evidence of deep love, or should I say, remnants of deep love.

In healthy relationships, couples will move in and out of intimacy without difficulty. With independent lives there is a healthy merging towards intimacy, then a drawing away to feel their unique separateness. When a couple becomes stuck in a cycle of conflict, however, the negative energy seems to gather momentum and becomes the focus of interest. Trust is lost, and even when one partner goes out of their way to fix the problem the effort is wasted in misconstrued motivation. It is quite difficult to take the heat out of the conflict, to bring each partner out of their self-absorbed perception of the situation to a point where they truly hear the other's point of view without diving into defensive reactions.

The separation of thought from feeling is critical, and couples often have to learn the difference. They have to learn to 'hold' and take in the nature of the other's feelings, rather than rushing into problem-solving or interpreting them as personal criticism. Learning to hold, rather than fix, is a common new learning. Only when you truly listen to each other can you begin to relate authentically and honestly with each other.

It seems that couples can put up with enormous amounts of conflict until a point is reached, or a line stepped over. I have seen relationships break up over the most seemingly insignificant actions, like a phone call that didn't come, or a single comment. It seems that we each hold certain aspects of our relationships as precious. For one, the tipping point might be loyalty. For another, respect, and another, trust. Couples will struggle on through tough issues like affairs, financial betrayal, dishonesty, and addiction, then suddenly there will be one slight nuance of a situation that prompts an overwhelming sense of it being too hard to continue.

I will hear statements like, 'I can't do this anymore', or, 'I know it seems silly, but that is it for me'. In this moment of truth it seems that all those aspects seen through those rose-coloured glasses suddenly become a shattered mess of broken faith and broken dreams. It is the loss of respect that brings commitment to an end, even for those who truly believed they would be committed for life. At the same time clients often express great sadness and loss of self-respect for turning away from their deeply held values of commitment. There appears to be a breaking point for everyone, some later than earlier. Once one partner has reached this breaking point there is very little willingness to resolve difficulties because respect has turned to resentment.

If good communication and a willingness to resolve any conflict has been built into the relationship there is a chance that this breaking point will not be reached. This willingness to resolve conflict needs to be present on a daily, weekly, and yearly basis. When the willingness is just not there anymore, the big task is to work out how to separate gracefully.

When the willingness to resolve conflict is absent, there comes a time when the relationship is at an end, at least in the form that it was. When there is a mature acceptance of the need to separate, friendship on some level often remains. If you each acknowledge that your personalities, wants, and lifestyles have not meshed sufficiently well to sustain the relationship, there is no need to enter into either self-blame, or blaming the other. It is a much healthier and more accurate perspective than saying anyone has failed in the relationship.

So much stress and emotional energy can be wasted on relationship breakups. Sometimes there is the cruel and gutless 'cutting-off' from all contact. At other times there are long and intense talks, tears, and heartfelt confessions that occupy days, nights, and dozens of text messages. While perseverance can be quite admirable, there is always a point at which it is obvious that the amount of hard work that has to be expended to keep the relationship operative is a sign in itself that the relationship is reaching its limits.

I admire those who know themselves well, who not only acknowledge their differences, but appreciate what has been gained from the time together as they part with respect and in friendship.

5
Secrets, and how to survive them

5.1. Sexual abuse, and beating shame

5.2. Trauma

5.3. Thriving instead of seeing yourself as a victim

5.1. Sexual abuse, and beating shame

You might hold secrets that might hurt someone else. You might hold secrets about things you have done that you regret. You might hold secrets to surprise someone, or you might hold secrets to protect yourself. Clearly it is the motivation behind the secret that determines whether it is healthy or destructive. In the case of sexual abuse, abusers often threaten their targets to make them stay silent. Targets of abuse often hold onto their secrets for many years. Shame and fear controls them until they reach a time in their life when they are sufficiently settled and confident in their emotional life that they feel comfortable in releasing their secret. When these kinds of secrets are buried emotionally, they tend to poison various aspects of living.

Regardless of your gender or sexual identity, the need for respectful behaviour underlies all relationships. When people abuse others, they overstep many boundaries. If you are tempted to act in a controlling way because you think you can get away with it, think again. No means no. The beliefs underlying that kind of abuse often lie in the notion that the other person is there for sexual use, gratification, or domination. If sexual interaction is outside the bounds of consensual intimacy, then it is abuse.

Just because you have the power to force yourself on someone else does not mean you have the right to do so, nor does getting someone drunk to make them compliant. Date-rape cannot be excused. Rape within a marriage or a partnership is also inexcusable. It is outside the bounds of consensual intimacy and common decency. It is immoral and illegal.

There are many traumas for those targeted with sexual abuse. A feeling of deep emotional pain arising from the loss of trust in others can be pervasive and long-lasting. Typically, children wrongly blame themselves for the abuse they experience. Those targeted by abuse can experience a wide range of emotions. For instance, there can be shame, a feeling of letting down parents, a need to protect family members from the truth, self-blame, and loathing. There can be anger towards parents for their lack of protection and parents will often blame themselves for not protecting their child.

Abusers know they are doing the wrong thing because they choose to abuse in private. When abusers are seductive, the target of the abuse is often left confused. Children especially will believe that they are to blame. Self-blame is futile. It plays into the power of the abuser and changes nothing. Responsibility needs to be directed at the abuser, the one who knew they were doing the wrong thing, the one who chose to do the wrong thing.

Clients who have been abused have often told me they feel damaged and unworthy. It is so tragic to hear this self-degradation when the abuser is the only one who should bear the pain of shame. Therapy work helps to redirect anger and look at the patterns of survival behaviour that have been adopted. Human beings are wonderful at finding ways to survive. They develop unique patterns of internal and external

5. Secrets, and how to survive them

behaviour that help them survive the immediate trauma and the ongoing demands of living. These survival patterns often continue into adult life and they are often beyond immediate awareness.

When patterns are positive and useful they often go unnoticed. When patterns are negative, they cause dysfunction. The skills that were once for survival are said to be 'past their use-by date'. They are no longer needed, and yet they pop up unwittingly. For instance, learning to withdraw from conflict might be a useful survival skill during abuse. Later in life it might result in needs not being met. Sadly, the impact of abuse is often insidious and far-reaching, the targets of the abuse struggling with fear of shame, loss of self-respect, anger and self-imposed guilt.

Shame lingers as long as secrets are held tightly. Shame can be a destructive force throughout your life if you don't acknowledge and dispute it. The cycle of abuse was often thought to perpetuate through generations, the perpetrator and the target unconsciously inheriting unhealthy belief systems from parents. This is no longer the case. Sexual abuse is openly discussed in our community and support is given to those who report abuse.

If you have suffered any kind of abuse, there is no need to dwell on feelings of shame. Accept them as an understandable reaction, but allow them to pass by quickly. There is no right or wrong way to feel, but if you find you are shaming yourself, be firm and confront this idea head on. You would not wish shame on your best friend, so don't do it to yourself. Talk about it, push it out of your existence. Be proud of who you are and how well you have survived.

There are other kinds of shame that are worth discussion. If you make an honest mistake with something, it is easy to shame yourself. A far healthier perspective is to accept your mistake as part of being human. Human error is taken into account in the statistics of every research project. It is accounted for. Rather than waste emotional energy on shaming yourself, face up to your mistakes, apologise, restore, and mend whatever you can, and forgive yourself while you put effort into making sure you don't make the same mistake again. If you have deliberately set out to do something wrong or have hurt someone, you will have to live with that shameful knowledge. Instead of feeling sorry for yourself, channel your shame into doing something to make amends to the person or community in whatever way you can. Show that you are sorry for what you have done rather than cower in self-pity or shame.

Speaking up to heal yourself
It is quite common for women not to disclose childhood abuse until they are in midlife, at a stage when they feel confident in their ability to cope. The confusion, shock, and conflict caused by abuse fragments and splits individuals into parallel experiences that are disconnected. Thoughts run along one track, feelings another, and the two often don't come together. The healing task is to become whole again, to be able to exist healthily in the here and now of each moment, to be able to blend thoughts and feelings when appropriate.

Young targets of abuse often have a huge fear that should they disclose abuse they will not be believed. For them, the ramifications of reporting take life into a totally unpredictable place. Mandatory reporting requires that anyone involved with young people have a legal obligation to report if they have any suspicion of child abuse. The objective is to stop any kind of abuse as soon as possible. This is a wonderfully protective message to the public, and has many benefits for abused children. If you are involved in reporting child abuse, you need to be ready for the fact that, in reality, it can also mean that the child may end up being removed from their family, temporarily or permanently. There is a possibility of the whole situation having a horrid outcome. It is so sad when this happens, because one trauma follows another. The process is unwieldy and unpredictable. However, if you refrain from reporting you are not only breaking the law but you are also allowing the abuse to perpetuate.

If you have personally experienced any kind of sexual abuse, early healing may mean learning to lay the blame and guilt where it belongs, instead of allowing it to poison your own self-esteem. It may mean striving to feel good about yourself through acknowledging what has happened, and refusing to feel like a victim. During sexual abuse, the target is seduced or made powerless, and choice is taken away. Learning to exercise your own personal power is critical to recovery. It is about taking back control of your life. Abusers try to win by overpowering and demeaning their victim. Make it your mission never to let the abuser win by holding you in fear of any kind. Rebuild your self-esteem if it needs it. Rebuild your confidence and power through loving yourself and being proud as you thrive rather than see yourself as a victim.

Under no circumstance in the healing process should self-esteem be compromised. In any kind of abuse there is an imbalance of power that puts the target of the abuse in a no-win situation. For some people, the process of taking back power involves having perpetrators charged. For others, when family relationships are at stake, healing can sometimes mean forgiveness and re-establishment of a workable relationship. You have to do what you need to do for you.

Having worked with many young men and women who have been targets of abuse, it has been clear to me that abuse affects individuals in many different ways. There seems little correlation between the severity of the abuse and the impact on the person. It is hideous to even think of trying to compare experience as being better or worse, yet it fascinates me the way resilience varies between personalities. I remember one teenager who had been gang-raped by some family members. She was strong-minded, sure of herself, and able to remain stable and balanced. I met her some years later and she had remained in control of her trauma.

In contrast, I recall a student who was traumatised when a male peer raised her skirt. That same student returned to the school as a student teacher and struggled emotionally to be back in that school environment because it reminded her of that boy's immature gesture. I have seen chronic abuse situations where mothers chose their husband over their child, rejecting the child, even when the husband has been incarcerated for the abuse. Individual responses to abuse can be quite horrifying.

People do heal from abuse and they do it in their own way. Traumatic experiences vary enormously in the effect they have on different individuals. If you are distressed by something that has happened to you, take it seriously and refrain from minimising the situation. Talk about it to as many people as possible. Seek help to work through whatever you need to work through.

5.2. Trauma

Trauma exists when you experience something out of the ordinary that shocks you. Your shock is a normal response to an abnormal situation. Falling over is the kind of passing trauma that is short-lived. Serious trauma tends to stay with you for the long-term, and often calls for special assistance.

Trauma responses can overwhelm you and causes your body to go into fight, flight, or freeze mode. Adrenaline floods your body and flows to your muscles to make them ready for quick action. Thought is bypassed because any thought distraction could prove dangerous by delaying your quick response. This is inherited from caveman days. The amygdala in your brain grab the blood, stopping its flow to the outer areas of the brain where decision-making takes place. You have no say in all this, your body takes over to help you survive. People often feel ashamed at the way they acted or failed to act while in survival mode, when in reality it was beyond their control.

I doubt anyone is immune from experiencing a trauma reaction, though individuals vary greatly in the way they experience trauma and in their ongoing resilience. We think of trauma being associated with war, assault, or natural disasters. Individuals suffer trauma in car accidents, seeing a loved one get hurt or collapse from a heart attack, or even going through an emergency medical procedure.

5. Secrets, and how to survive them

Trauma is not over quickly; it stays with you. Some can experience ongoing stress symptoms like hypervigilance, hyperarousal, body sensations, and triggered reactions to sense data like noise or smell. There are a myriad of other typical reactions that are uncomfortable and uncontrollable in the short-term. Triggers might cause you to withdraw, feel numb, or to act out and become angry.

It is the telling and retelling of your story over and over again that helps you desensitise yourself so that the experience eventually seems less traumatic. If something traumatic happens to you, don't hold back from telling others. Tell family and friends what happened. The more times you tell the story, the quicker you will become accustomed to it – however, telling the story too soon may have the effect of re-traumatising you. It is about rebuilding resilience, one step at a time.

Shutting away any emotional response or refusing to acknowledge the trauma can lead to ongoing ill health. When people respond like this it is important that they are encouraged to speak about their experience at their own pace, and in their own time. For some it comes naturally, sharing with family and friends. In other families there is a 'stiff upper lip' policy that demands grief and emotion be put aside, a sense that talking about it makes it worse. Of course, there needs to be a balance in this. There will be times when the traumatised person will feel like talking and times when they won't. If there is no avenue for talking within the family, it is critical that outside professional support is obtained.

For some, the mere news of a critical event quite unrelated to them may also raise a traumatic reaction. Vicarious trauma is something you experience from time to time as you listen to the daily news. There is shock, disbelief, panic, and an 'it could have been me' type of thinking. Those experiencing vicarious trauma can sometimes lock their emotion away with a sense of guilt that it didn't happen to them. People suffering from vicarious trauma also need to talk about what they are feeling.

For people who are victims of trauma, therapeutic work in this area involves creating a calm and safe place where clients can ever so gradually extend their comfort zone, gradually challenging themselves to regain their confidence in the affected area of their lives. It is about holding and nurturing emotionally. It is about teaching the client to self-regulate, to be aware of their body reactions, and to work with them to remain calm and in control. Therapeutic work is not about brutal return to the trauma. It is never wise to ask trauma victims to go back to the time of the trauma and tell you exactly what happened. This is re-traumatising, unless it is something that is initiated by the trauma victim.

With any trauma comes a sense of disempowerment and the loss of feeling safe and secure. Regaining a sense of power is a gradual experience. Encourage simple decision-making from the start like, 'Would you like me to take you to ...', or, 'Would you like a glass of water, or would you prefer a cup of tea?' This helps the traumatised person start to regain some power over their environment, and healing begins as the traumatised person begins to take back control of their life. Direct and reassuring eye contact brings people back into the reality of contact with another. If appropriate, seek permission before touching or consoling. This will not be appropriate in cases of assault.

It is also important to know that when dealing with anyone who has experienced trauma, it is important to ensure that they feel safe at all times. Nurturing environments are needed to provide the kind of support necessary for recovery. Remember, when emotions are expressed you will move through them to a different set of emotions. It has to be gradual.

If you fear that someone is too emotionally locked up after a traumatic incident, you can ask some peripheral questions to broaden the context of the event, like, 'How did you get in touch with your mum?', or, 'Where was your partner at the time?' This helps to broaden out the person's memory of the event and draws them out of the memory corridor that leads to the horrific memories.

5. Secrets, and how to survive them

Any good trauma brochure will detail the ongoing signs of trauma responses that need to be looked out for and taken notice of, such as flashbacks.

What often troubles people months down the track are recurrent nightmares. The brain seems to process by night what is too hard to deal with during the day, and tries to make sense of our daily experience. According to gestalt theory, each part of your dream represents disowned aspects of yourself. Invariably, when attention is paid to dreams during therapy it leads to an astonishing absence of them by night.

It is not only *what* happens to you, but *how* you react to your experience that determines your level of trauma. We have no idea what traumas our children will experience. We can't protect them every minute of the day. Modelling resilience and perseverance rather than learned helplessness is the greatest gift you can give your children.

Resilience, perseverance, and determination makes children strong in the face of, and in the aftermath of trauma. Resilient children have some innate protection from the devastation that trauma might otherwise cause. The stronger they are, the better, whereas learned helplessness teaches children to be victims. It makes them sitting ducks for abusers who skilfully seek out those who are vulnerable. If children learn to catastrophise what happens to them, they are in trouble if they start to indulge in victim thinking.

With any traumatic experience, we can never say that it didn't happen. Being resilient means that you deliberately choose to look at the cup as half-full. You choose to pick yourself up and persevere in your search for ways to make your situation better, however big or small that may be. The less healthy choice is to cower, to blame individuals or the world in general for your situation, and to be forever at the mercy of benevolence, rather than your own internal resilient resources.

5.3. Thriving, instead of seeing yourself as a victim

World leaders spoke out after 9/11, proclaiming a refusal to live like victims after the attack that changed the world. What were they talking about? A victim stance attempts to draw others into sympathy, support, and doing things for you. It is about feeling sorry for yourself, or feeling forever damaged. Feeling like a victim is disempowering and becomes a self-fulfilling prophecy. Choosing to be a victim provides a convenient way to avoid having to take responsibility for the effort that is needed to rebuild your life. The cost of choosing this stance is subtle and often overlooked by people in the midst of trauma recovery.

Insidiously, victim thinking can take over your personality and damage your self-esteem. It creates distance with others who see very quickly that their efforts of support are wasted because the victim is hell-bent on believing the rest of the world is out to make their life difficult. Victim thinking has an element of 'the world owes me'. Victim thinking makes for a very difficult and lonely life. It can lead to poor attachment and overprotective parenting.

Victims stop themselves from daring to dream because they predict they will be thwarted. They mourn their situation in life and have little faith in themselves to rise above their misery. The look to others to fix it for them. It is much more than a lack of resilience. It is a reluctance to dream, to risk, to move forward in a positive way, or to celebrate your own success.

In times of trauma, adults often struggle to draw on their resilience and strength. Even competent and well-balanced adults can be pushed to the limit of their resilience. Exposure to trauma can compound unless it is taken seriously. If you are working in high-risk areas, it is foolish to deny debriefing or counselling support. I frequently meet high-functioning clients who are dumbfounded that they have been rocked by a particular traumatic event. In their minds they have dealt with plenty of similar situations and have never previously been affected. Suddenly, they find themselves really shaken by a situation that has never troubled them in the past.

5. Secrets, and how to survive them

Trauma at work
Adults often expect to deal with trauma in a routine way. They try to problem-solve it. Many have special jobs where trauma is inherent. Firefighters, for instance, are pretty tough individuals who have my total admiration, yet even they have their limits in managing trauma, as do those in the armed forces. To refuse to be impacted by a shocking trauma is not good sense, because serious trauma is not an everyday occurrence. There is wisdom in acknowledging when you have been affected by a traumatic experience, and also in admitting you need assistance to move you to an emotional place of safety where you feel well supported.

It is important to be able to minimise any tendency to further traumatise yourself. I recall a senior police officer who had spent many years attending traffic accidents. His trauma was not the gruesome sights he saw but the imagined impact on the families and loved ones who bore the trauma personally. Years later, his thought patterns had led him to imagine the impact on their lives over a long period of time. He was re-traumatising himself with imagined trauma. Who knows what kinds of lives those individuals had been able to lead? To imagine that you know their pathway is to live in a world of fantasy, a self-made nightmare in his case.

Professional workers exposed to constant trauma need strong emotional limits. This means knowing their own personal issues and being dedicated to seeking assistance when a crossover starts to happen that puts the them in danger of losing emotional boundaries. This occurs when they become confused between what they are feeling for themselves and what they are imagining the affected others are feeling. It requires dedication to remaining focused on one's own personal life, rather than the lives and suffering of those dealt with on a daily basis. It requires understanding where your own emotional response has come from and what has triggered it to pop up at a particular time, or in response to a particular trauma situation.

Regular debriefing is essential to ongoing good mental health. When symptoms of post-traumatic stress occur, it is important to surround yourself by a comfortable and safe environment. Gradually, as you recover you will be able to expand your degree of tolerance for situations that are less safe and less predictable. As you recover you have to meet the randomness of the world, and it really helps to have a professional support to recover your confidence before you make plans for a graduated return to work.

Rebuilding resilience

Life is full of experiences. Sometimes they are wonderful, sometimes they are horrendous. Life does happen. Imagine a life where nothing bad ever happened, where we had everything we wanted ... how boring and meaningless life would be. It is the ups and downs of life that make this experience, that teach our children that they have the strength to endure the difficult parts. Over-protection leads to vulnerability. Children need to find their own resilience, rather than be 'untouched' by life. When children are over protected, it sets them up for an everlasting battle within themselves, a feeling that life has dealt them a bad hand with every discomfort that comes along. It trains them for victim thinking. Remember, it is not the crisis that counts, but the way in which you handle it that determines the quality of your chosen life pathway. Resilience is a choice that brings rewards.

If you have been the target of any kind of abuse, know that you are not alone. You have a choice to give in, to be bitter and angry, and diminish your sense of self-worth. This only fuels your abuser's power and control. I encourage you to step outside that kind of thinking. Choose not to be a victim. Choose to celebrate yourself and your ability to survive. Know that you can learn to trust again because your 'crap radar' has been heightened. Why should you diminish your self-esteem, especially when you have not done a thing wrong? Find strength in your capacity to survive, and build a healthy life. Love yourself and use your deepened understanding of life to fuel your passion for what you believe in. Turn pain into joy. Turn bitterness into love and positive energy. Use your anger to fuel your growth in resilience.

6

Emotional intelligence in the workplace

- 6.1. *Becoming a manager*
- 6.2. *Working alongside other managers*
- 6.3. *Dealing with difficult personalities*
- 6.4. *Having hard conversations with those you supervise*
- 6.5. *Work/life balance*
- 6.6. *When those you supervise have special skills*
- 6.7. *Working under higher management*

6.1. Becoming a manager

Whether it is in casual employment that accompanies your study path, or in full-time career employment, the first promotion is challenging on many levels. Starting at the bottom of any organisation has its advantages because it gives you the opportunity to observe how people in those management positions conduct themselves. You may have the opportunity to stand in for your manager on a short-term basis. This is a challenging situation when you are suddenly in charge of your co-workers knowing that you will resume your position alongside them at the end of your term as acting manager.

When you are required to make tough decisions, make it clear that your decisions have to be made in the best interests of the organisation, not your friends. By all means apologise if your co-workers feel let down, but don't apologise for the decision. True friends and colleagues will understand your position and admire you for a fair decision, however, there are always a variety of personalities who will react in different ways. As a manager, it is hard to make everyone happy.

The workplace is a challenging environment where you are brought into contact with people very different to yourself. The old saying that, 'You can choose your friends but not your relatives' can be extended to 'your workmates'. Survival in an organisation often means being capable of getting along with people you would not normally choose to mix with out of work hours. Being a manager in a work environment often requires you to step back and command the best from the workers under you, as well as work cooperatively with other managers. You need to go out of your way to get to know all of them. If you start your own business, you will find it will be up to you to motivate your staff. You may also find that you suddenly become confidante for staff in trouble in their private lives. It goes with the territory.

Your first job as a new manager
It can be quite daunting if you have to walk into a management role where there are 'old hands' who have been in their position for years. It is a natural first response to feel defensive. The trouble is if you react in a defensive way you will be inclined to devalue the experience of the old hands as a means of bolstering your own confidence. A negative cycle begins.

While you, as a new young manager, puddle around trying to learn the job that the oldies know through and through, the old hands are likely to become increasingly frustrated and feel their opinion is not valued. No doubt they see all the pitfalls that you are heading for, but without a respectful avenue to put their point across, they will say nothing. They are likely to imagine that should they speak up, they will be seen as an undermining personality. This kind of thinking makes it easy for them to stand back and enjoy an, 'I told you so' when the moment of disaster hits.

Get to them first. Seek their opinion upfront. A sharp young manager will take time to talk with as many workers as possible and question them about existing negatives, and the things they are keen to change. Appeal to their creative side by asking, 'How can we do this better?', or, 'Do you have any suggestions?' These kinds of questions have every chance of bringing the old hands on board with change. Listen to their responses carefully. Let them know you have heard their point of view. Refer back to them when you make your decisions. Where possible give them your reasons. Be open and honest when you are unsure of the best pathway but be firm in your decision-making. Don't be afraid to be authoritative in your approach, but be respectful and they will come on board with your journey.

There will always be some negative personalities. Beware the classic comment, 'If it ain't broke, don't fix it'. This is often used to block creative change, though it can also reflect an underlying aspect of the good things that are currently happening that should not be cast aside. It is worth taking the time to understand the underlying fears and strong points of view. Change has to be implemented in a way that staff understand and know what to expect. They have to see real benefit in the end point of the change, and even better, some benefits that they will experience personally. Higher profit margins don't cut it unless there is some personal benefit to be gained.

What is it that workers value in a manager?
Juniors value fairness and honesty of the kind often experienced growing up in the school system. Juniors do not take kindly to managers who play favourites, or managers who target or belittle people unfairly. They really struggle and often feel inadequate or shamed because they are not measuring up to, or impressing their first-ever boss. Juniors need looking after,

or at least their self-esteem needs nurturing. Make sure you treat juniors with respect and kindness. Give them a strong guiding hand in terms of what is expected of them. Help them transition from school to work by gradually showing them what is expected. Role model good work behaviour. They will catch on, but not all at once. Joking or belittling juniors at their expense is not on. Harassment only produces long-term resentment and loss of productivity. If there is one thing I know about teenagers, they are very quick at 'crap detecting' and seeing you for who you really are. They will pick up on negative or bullying type attitudes fast.

Young employees who have had positive experiences in other jobs tend to leave quickly when they encounter a manager or supervisor who is a bully. When older employees complain about the 'boss from hell' they have often exerted so much energy with their disgust over the boss's behaviour that they become exhausted and emotionally drained. They often try harder to make the job work for them, using personal discipline to try to be immune to the bully. When anyone encounters this kind of boss it takes considerable maturity to handle the situation without behaving poorly in response. It makes no difference if you are a junior, a young person, or a senior manager – a manager who bullies will take a huge toll on every employee's health, wellbeing, and production capabilities.

Most adults have some experience of having to work with a manager for whom they hold little respect. It is critical that poor management is identified for what it is. Too often bullied employees start to accept the bullying behaviour as normal, and believe they are being personally targeted. Loss of confidence and self-esteem is inevitable regardless of age or experience. It takes an emotionally strong person to withstand ongoing harassment without having one's self-esteem assaulted. It is simply not worth it!

Training your team
It is the first and most important tenet of education that you must start where the learner is at. From there, if you encourage and value the positive aspects of a person's good effort and

behaviour, the learner will be more likely to respect you and more likely to work on any deficits. If you choose to focus on the negative aspects of an employee's performance, you will find that things get worse. If there is a long list of behaviours that need to change, keep up positive reinforcement for what is going well, and choose only one or two behaviours from the list that the employee needs to focus on.

If an employee is failing with a task, you may have missed something in his or her training. Retrace the training, step-by-step, starting from the beginning. Go over routines and processes with them. Explain the importance of each core task and what will go wrong if they make a mistake. Remember, everyone learns in different ways. Ask the trainee if it helps to write things down for them, or if they would prefer a diagram, or some further observation training. Never assume that because you have explained it once that they should get it. The art of teaching lies in the way the learner receives the message. It is not until the message is fully-received that your job as teacher or trainer is done.

If you are a new manager, you may have new ideas and new perspectives on what needs to change or develop. Hold these until you have built trust and cooperation with your team. Change has to be managed carefully. Take time to chat and listen to what your workers think. Bring together their ideas and have the humility to let them have ownership of some of the changes, rather than taking kudos yourself. Your humility will bring huge rewards in the form of respect. They will gain in self-worth and will be more energetic in implementing the changes.

6.2. Working alongside other managers

As a new manager you will most likely have to work alongside other managers. Some will be a joy, others may be difficult. With luck you will have a team that gets along well and provides a strong support structure for you. Where there are difficulties, realise that the difficult personalities are likely to be the ones who are a little more insecure in some way, though their exterior paints another picture. They may push themselves forward to be in a good light, or use emotional manipulation to get what they want. They may be scathing of your enthusiasm and energy. Be wary of subtle emotional manipulation. It can be quite daunting, and can catch you off guard.

I recall a couple of 24-year-olds who were distressed at the antics of one of their fellow workers who had previously been a friend. The workmate they described maintained a victim mentality and interpreted every action by others with paranoia. They were frightened that she would do something to herself if they didn't go along with her requests. They helped her seek support, they swapped shifts, changed the share of duties, and were in a constant state of shock that she could still feel miserable, thankless, and hard-done by.

What they could not see was that by walking on tippy toes around her they were maintaining her problem behaviour. She was expert at emotional blackmail, and they were enabling her by being so helpful. These 24-year-olds had to be coached to acknowledge their own hurt and to find the appropriate words to say in order to remove themselves from the friendship. Simply stated, they needed to tell their workmate that they had been extremely hurt by her emotional manipulations, that she appeared to have no appreciation of their assistance, and that they were not prepared to put themselves out for her again. They had to accept the fact that their workmate may become defensive, sulky, and may even lash out verbally.

The important thing is to express what needs to be said in a polite and respectful way, rather than unexpectedly lash out in an undisciplined way. These folk had to learn that how their workmate responds is a function of her ability to take responsibility for her actions, or not. It takes good interpersonal skills to handle a situation like this. At best, there might be an opening up of real communication, and a new start to a more open and honest dialogue. At worst, the workmate might sink deeper into victim behaviours.

6.3. Dealing with difficult personalities

Rather than react to difficult personalities, make it your personal challenge to observe, get along with, and get the best out of those personalities, putting your negative perceptions and dislikes aside. If you over-focus on one annoying behaviour, then the catastrophising of the behaviour is likely to cloud your judgement. The emotionally intelligent pathway is to look beyond specific traits to understand the deeper complexities in the irritating personality. Searching out one likeable trait or interest in common will build a positive bridge to improvements in the areas of concern.

Difficult personalities in the workplace will challenge you to be canny about the way you conduct yourself. The workplace is a different environment to other social groupings. In social relationships you can walk away at will. In a work environment it is necessary to persist with the relationship and to do everything you can to make it work.

It can be quite difficult to work out where another person is coming from emotionally. The real underlying issue may not be present in the behaviour that you see. Human beings are often quite complicated. They will deliberately push someone away when the opposite is what they really want. They can smile on the surface and carry resentment underneath.

It is possible to use the experience of your own emotion to gain clues to underlying emotion in others. When you suddenly become aware that you are absorbing or picking up emotion from another person, you are experiencing what is called transference. Transference operates in many human interactions. You can become happy when you are with a happy person. You can feel unusually heavy when you are with a depressed person. You can react with hostility when you are with a hostile person. You can feel downcast when you are with someone with low self-esteem. Apathy is likely to engender apathy in you.

If you are unaware of the emotion that has been transferred or absorbed by you, you are likely to react in kind. If this is a negative emotion you are likely to make the situation worse. On the other hand, if you take notice of the transference you experience you will be able to step back, take stock of your own emotion, and to think about how you might respond in a way that will reduce negative emotion in the other person. It gives you a chance to act in a way that moves the other person to a more positive place, rather than exacerbating the discord between you. Remember, the goal here is to get the best out of this difficult worker.

Themes underlying difficult behaviour
Behaviour can be quite predictable once you work out a person's likely life theme. There are those who are always expecting to be hurt by someone. They have probably grown up with mistrust and abuse. Those who always need someone to help them have probably grown up feeling helpless. Those who exclude themselves socially do so because they feel different, and feel like they never belong because they could never fit in with groups. Those who are particularly vulnerable have often known fear and disaster in their lives.

Some people expect to fail because they have lots of failures, while others are consumed with being helpful and trying to please others because they are used to sacrificing their own needs. Some have very high standards and work relentlessly to achieve them, whereas other feel fake, internally flawed, and defective. They expect a lot of themselves and others. Of course, there are also those who feel entitled. They see themselves as special and deserving of the best.

In competitive environments, try to identify those personalities driven for power and determined to achieve it, regardless of the cost. Be alert to the unspoken reactions of others and the behind-the-scenes game playing. Those driven by power, rather than humility, can be quite subtle in their destruction. Know that you are easily set up with one side of any story. Be wary of those who are forthright in speaking badly of others. It is so easy for them to create a picture in your mind of one of their co-workers. Always look beyond the story presented to you. Seek out all kinds of information. Take account of first-hand interactions and be astute to those personalities who may be nice to your face but demeaning behind your back. Identify those you can trust.

When there is a difficult personality to be negotiated, it is important to act within your own integrity, to be true to yourself, and to be clear and authentic in your communication with others. Rather than retaliate, keep your own behaviour at a professional level. Eventually the difficult personality will step over the line. Games of sabotage are designed to provoke retaliation, which then gives substance to lodging a grievance against you. It can get very messy. Without retaliation, the game player has no ammunition. Eventually they become so outraged that their own self-esteem comes under attack. Lack of retaliation becomes a reminder to them of their own weakness. It highlights their own lack of professionalism.

To handle difficult personalities, a carefully constructed mindset is required. It is so easy to rush into defence mode when challenged. It takes considerable restraint in a situation where you receive a verbal lashing. Hostility breeds hostility, and it is hard not to react to it accordingly. It is a natural reaction, but it does not help in any situation; it puts you directly into the hands of the bully. It weakens your position and inflates the offender's position.

If you can remain calm and control your response, this puts the offender on the back foot. Eventually, the offender will start to appear ridiculous, even to him or herself.

Conflict resolution
When there is a fundamental difference of opinion, conflict can grow to become explosive and divisive in the workplace. De-escalating the conflict requires that you identify when employees enter a defensive mode. Be direct and give confidence that the issue can be sorted.

Step back and allow the person to vent their feelings without any reaction from you. Give non-threatening directives e.g. 'I need you to come inside and sit down where we can talk about this'. Let the person know that you understand how upset they are. Be firm on the things you need to be firm about. If the person remains noncompliant, set the limits and redirect the person's focus. Distract them if you can. Monitor the safety of the area and the people in close proximity. If the situation intensifies with intimidation and threats, take this seriously. Call for help, use a panic button, or make an indication to someone to call the police.

The enraged person will eventually calm down and start to ask questions to which you need to give direct responses. Downplay any challenge made to you, stick to the topic, and refrain from being sucked into the hostility. Stay calm yourself and keep comments factual. Put a lid on your resentment.

If the person is not abusive but is just distressed, give them privacy, care, and concern. Offer to call someone close to them, or to help them get home. If someone is behaving in a socially unacceptable way, leave them alone and remove other people from the area. As the tension reduces, you will see a drop in energy. Indicate your goodwill in sorting out the issue. Establish rapport and be caring towards the person.

There is a natural progression and winding down that occurs when someone is involved in conflict. If you do not see a natural winding down as the person expresses their hurt or distress, be alert to whether this is a narcissistic rant where you feel intimidated, or if there is some sense of a drug influence. With a narcissistic rant, the person has absolutely no regard for the way the message is being received. There is no consideration for the fact that the delivery is terrifying someone else. It is like a barrage of abuse that does not stop and it is extremely uncomfortable, frightening and disturbing to be the target of something like this. Nothing you say or do will make much difference to the person doing the ranting. Call for support immediately because this person is not responding in a normal manner, and it is likely their behaviour will continue to escalate.

Formal conflict resolution

If you have a situation where there is a conflict that needs to be resolved between two staff, it may be necessary to set up formal mediation to arrive at a resolution. Give yourself time to set this up. Prepare dot points of what you know of each side of the conflict after interviewing each person. Identify what they expect out of the mediation, but most importantly, ascertain their willingness to come to some compromise. Each participant needs to accept that their points of view are in such opposition that neither is likely to gain exactly what they want. That is the point of mediation, to come to a reasonable compromise.

During the mediation, give time for each to have their say. Demand that they use 'I' language, and own their opinions rather than be finger pointing or using 'you' language in a judgemental way. With mediation, once each participant hears the other's point of view there is usually a greater understanding and appreciation of the other's true motivation, dispelling the previously held fantasy that the other person is a 'monster.'

The mediation has more chance of success if there is a negative consequence that arises for both if they fail to resolve the conflict. As the mediation unfolds and a compromise is reached, make sure you write down word-for-word what has been agreed to, and ask each to sign for validation of their agreement. The situation needs following up further down the track, to ensure the welfare of both parties.

If either participant is not willing to resolve the conflict through compromise, there is no point in running a mediation.

6.4. Having hard conversations with those you supervise

Whether it is an employee who is doing the wrong thing, or a particularly difficult personality, it is counterproductive to allow yourself to go into a defensive mode, to act like you are a victim or react in an aggressive or bullying way. It requires humility to take unfair criticism without becoming hostile, and it takes tactful cunning to move the person criticising you to a more positive perspective. Reality is sometimes hard to hear.

Take time formulating hard conversations. Plan what you would say, and try to think in an emotionally intelligent way that pays regard to the emotional wellbeing of the person you will be talking to. As you start to think about the situation, begin with some introspective examination. To what extent has this person got under your skin, and to what extent have you perceived their actions as personal criticism, and are carrying hostility towards them? Can you have this hard conversation without letting your personal annoyance and frustration colour the interview? To what extent have you been beating yourself up because you have not been able to succeed in getting this person onside? Once you have completed this internal assessment, look at the situation in a scientific way. What have you observed, what are the facts, what are your expectations and what are your requirements?

The nature of the discussion you have with workers is critical to the amount of positive change that eventuates. There are several educational principles that have been tested and tried in education settings. These are worth keeping in mind. Understand that growth and learning take place when an individual experiences success. Try to support, encourage, and provide appropriate learning tools. Acknowledge effort and small successes. When there is a multitude of deficits, develop a graduated plan that starts with positive change in one or two behaviours. This success can then be used as a springboard to effect change in other areas. Start with the most achievable.

Preparing for a hard conversation
1. After completing your own introspective examination, make sure you have control of any personal angst. These must be put aside in order for you to address the situation in an unbiased, scientific way.

6. Emotional intelligence in the workplace

2. Find an appropriate time and place to have this hard conversation. It is not acceptable to berate someone in front of their peers.
3. Prepare a clear statement of what you intend to say. You need to take a stance based on observations and data, not innuendo or emotional perception. Have your facts right. Remember that no one responds well to negative barrages uttered in a judgemental way. A wise employer or team leader will take time to acknowledge positive aspects of the employee's behaviour before focusing on what needs improvement. Criticism will always be received better when there is genuine acknowledgement of personal strengths. This may mean thoughtful preparation and true soul-searching to find redeeming features. This will be time well-spent, and may mean the difference between genuine positive change, and vengeful sabotage. E.g. 'You do a great job serving the youngsters who come in here'.
4. Explain the behaviour that is inappropriate or causing concern. Just because you think the problem is obvious, this may not be the case with the employee. Ask the employee to help you understand the situation leading to the problem, e.g. 'I am keen for this place to be as efficient as possible. I have noticed that you have been late into work five times in the last six shifts. Can you tell me what the problem is that is making you late?'
5. High expectations are important. It is important to explain in a clear and concise manner the behaviours that need to be achieved, however, with high expectations comes a huge responsibility to make wise assessments of what is achievable. Performance indicators that are constantly raised regardless of the emotional commitment made by the individual will only serve to produce burnout,

feelings of failure, and long-term expense in recruitment and training. It is not helpful to the individual or the organisation in the long-term to expect ever increasing performance targets. Articulate reasonable expectation and clearly outline the consequences of poor choices.
6. Enforce consequences and validate positive effort.

6.5. Work/life balance

It is sad to see some young managers who have burnt out from the effort of being upwardly mobile. They swallow whole the mission and ideals of their organisation, and become adept at wearing the correct organisational mask. Away from work, these same young managers often battle with issues like depression, separation, addiction, or eating disorders. They can be fully-functioning in one aspect of their life, though miserably confused in other aspects as the drive to climb the corporate ladder consumes their sense of balance. They sometimes see themselves as having grown beyond their partner, and sometimes even choose not to share their newfound obsession. To begin with, they have a sense of 'having arrived' in the next status echelon. The 'we' becomes an 'I'. It is unfortunate that they fail to see that it is the humility they have lost that would ultimately allow them to become really high fliers. They soon find that they are living to work, rather than working to live. Before long they find they are hooked into a particular status/level because their ego has turned them into something akin to a robot and they lack the personal qualities required for management positions.

In this situation, therapeutic work involves assisting individuals to reconnect firstly with themselves, and then with others. There is often a dilemma for management. How do they determine which employees need to be given the organisational 'pitch' several times over, and which ones are likely to swallow the corporate message as gospel? How do they identify the employees who will rush to join the crusade, leaving social wreckage in their wake? Savvy employers do not like to see employees carried away with a focus on performance targets and the company mission. Employers know that something has to give and it always does. Often, the bright young star climbing quickly to the top becomes a fallen star, with family breakup, affairs, addictions, nervous breakdowns, etc.

While there is no getting away from the organisational objective of profit and competition, training programs need to focus more on the perfection of work/life balance. Endless increases in performance targets are designed to destroy. It is not rocket science! The constant striving to do better is what causes burnout. There needs to be a culture in which workers are validated for their own unique contributions, whatever they be. They could take a leaf from educational settings and understand that the key to individual productivity in the workforce hinges on a sense of belonging, personal validation, teamwork and personal balance.

6.6. When those you supervise have special skills

Increasing fields of specialisation means that it is common for workers with special skills to be managed by someone who does not have their skillset. A key to their productivity lies in motivating them to stay on task, and to become efficient producers. Each of these workers is likely to gain something different from their work. For one, the motivating factor might be promotion and financial gain; another might simply be love for the artistry in their work. You won't know unless you take time to talk with your workers to identify not only their skills and talents, but their motivations and enjoyment factors present in their daily work.

As their manager, the onus is on you to behave with integrity; to be competent in your own field, and to show respect for your workers' unique skillsets. This is especially true in risky areas where the potential for human error is greater. Once you show your workers that you are keen to learn from them, the whole dynamic changes. They become part of your team, your support, and your knowledge base. This is not to say that they won't make mistakes, but those working under you will feel more secure and positive in their efforts if they know you will back them when things go wrong, that you will understand and trust that they do not deliberately make mistakes.

If, on the other hand, you choose to take an autocratic rule over your workers, they will come to anticipate that you will not support them if they make a mistake. If you behave in this way, you will find the rate of their mistakes is likely to increase. A more positive or supportive response will bring their ongoing loyalty, and your workers will most likely work harder to make sure it doesn't happen again. They won't want to let you down.

If you are open and truthful, fair in your dealings, and make your expectations clear, you will find that your workers will respect you. Where workers have unique expertise, they also need to be recognised as having exclusive responsibility that is granted to them through respect and appreciation. If the relationship is working, the motivational aspect will be gained through respect for you and your management style.

6.7. Working under higher management

Unless you are working in your own business, there is a good chance that you will have one or more managers above you. You may feel appreciated and encouraged by their comments as there are many managers who have an instinctive understanding of how to treat their team decently. They let you know what they expect in a way that encourages, rather than stresses you. Performance reviews take an objective look at your achievements, your strengths, and your weaknesses.

If you have your performance under review because there is a problem, be open and honest about any difficulties you are experiencing. No employee is perfect and it is essential to own any inadequate behaviour, and to do something to rectify the situation. When criticism does not seem to fit with you, take some time out to think it all through. While it is important to own your own inadequacies or mistakes, it is also essential to reject, at least in your own mind, any criticism that can honestly be said to result from an employer's lack of skill as a manager. It may be wise to keep this insight to yourself in the first instance. You will have to read the situation and the particular personality to gauge whether there is any point in discussing the issues. The important thing is how you feel about yourself. If you know the criticism is unjustified, then bide your time. Ask for a second interview after you have had time to prepare your case. Try to problem-solve and plan how you might address the situation in a clever way so that your boss comes to realise his own error of judgement. Never, ever, allow your self-esteem to be depleted by a manager who has poor management skills. I cannot say that strongly enough.

If you are clear about what constitutes professional behaviour then you can acknowledge that not all managers are perfect, and that you do have choices.

1. You can choose to live with the issue (without wasting personal energy).
2. You can be assertive and simply state your preference for how you would like to be treated.
3. You can assertively seek out appropriate channels to lodge an official complaint.
4. You can look elsewhere for work.

If, on the other hand, criticism comes from a manager who has your full respect, then perhaps you would be wise to step back and consider your manager's perspective. Analyse the changes you need to make, and have a conviction to alter whatever needs to be altered. For instance, you might think you are being friendly to customers, but your employer might say you appear surly. What you think is not necessarily the reality from another's perspective.

If you have the misfortune of having an unreasonable manager who lashes out, has some personality disorder, or is insecure, you will find that you need to use every ounce of maturity that you can muster. It is so important to protect yourself emotionally. Think about why this person is behaving in an unreasonable way. What is the weakness underneath that is their driving force? What is it that they are trying to achieve, e.g. big-noting, attention, power, or vengeance? Like naughty children, once you know what the aim of the behaviour is, the more chance you have of catering for that need in a way that is not personally destructive. Once you have worked that out, you will be able to find ways to settle or reassure your employer.

Remember your experience as an employee. Don't sweep issues aside thinking that now you are a manager you have to 'act' a different role. Certainly you will have more responsibilities, but trust your instinct as to how you preferred to be treated as an employee. Remember that workers appreciate being treated fairly, and they like their manager to be positive about their efforts and caring about them as individuals. Most team members will respect your position as manager, and the majority understand that everyone benefits from being part of a cooperative team. Most will go out of their way to assist you in whatever way you need. Value their willingness.

7

Creating family

> 7.1. Sustaining relationships over the long-term
> 7.2. Violence, anger, possession, and paranoia ... power and control

7.1. Sustaining relationships over the long-term

Relationships need work

You might be lucky enough to meet your childhood sweetheart and live together happily ever after, however, people grow and change as they move into adulthood, and this can make it difficult to sustain relationships established in teenage years. Once children come along, it sometimes happens that one partner develops new interests while the other is more caught up with being the primary child carer, growing in lots of ways, but not developing interests outside family life. Life events challenge sound relationships. Any glitch in communication can easily become wider and wider unless the issues are addressed when they first become evident. It requires conscious work to keep communication happening.

If you have experienced a number of broken relationships, the prospect of trusting again is probably quite daunting. There is complexity in relationships, and there should be no shame in admitting worries about things going wrong. One couple was so open about their fear that they attended regular sessions just to make sure they were addressing everything that needed to be addressed. They regarded the counselling session as simple maintenance for their relationship. For this couple, therapy gave space for the development of a new and deeper dimension, a place where they could get into the habit of addressing the difficult topics.

If you and your partner can have regular chats about how the relationship is going, that is great. If you really struggle to have this kind of conversation then make sure you enlist some support from a professional counsellor. If you bite your tongue in fear of upsetting the other, or just hope the issues will go away, you are likely to find them loom bigger than ever. With or without counselling support, you as a couple need to persist with your communication to ensure you have a team approach to every issue, whether they be surface ripples or deeper issues that are difficult to talk about. Your lives need to revolve around a 'we', rather than just two 'I's'.

If your relationship is healthy, neither you, nor your partner, will be subservient or dominating. You will each have your own solid identity. You will each like, respect, and love the other. These may sound like platitudes, but in reality they form the essentials required to sustain your relationship over the long-term. If your relationship is tumultuous, don't fall into the trap of thinking that because poor behaviour has been forgiven, it has also been forgotten. There are only a certain number of times that poor behaviour will be forgiven. Resentment creeps in with each incident. It builds until one day some small crisis becomes a deal-breaker and the relationship crumbles.

If your family relationships work well there is likely to be a sharing of the load; physically, mentally, and emotionally. Each of you will be contributing and drawing on the energy of the other. Each of you will take the initiative to contribute to the present and future directions of the partnership. There will be consideration and respect for the part that each of you plays in the family, and there will be honest, healthy, and productive discussion over any straying from your family's code of behaviour. There is great fun to be had in planning the future together, as well as enjoying the present. Life may not necessarily be easy, but there are always things to look forward to individually, in partnership, and as a family. The catch is, these things take effort to organise.

Challenge your certainties

As individuals grow and find their place in the world they become increasingly confident about their views on life and politics. It is wonderful if you are able to share your views with your partner without it ending up in heightened argument which puts stress on your relationship. If you can, it means you have each learned to agree to differ.

If you are both strong personalities who clash regularly and are unable to agree to disagree, conflict is likely to continue. This can place your relationship in jeopardy. Having to be right or having to win is a definite relationship downer. If this happens in your relationship, understand that you are forgetting the big picture in which you each have a right to an opinion, but it is your own opinion; you cannot force it on someone else. Understand that while it may be relatively easy to win an argument, it is a lot harder to keep your partner's respect.

Convincing yourself you are right about anything can lead you down a dangerous pathway, one in which you can experience such a high because you are so caught up in the ride of being right that you miss the facts to the contrary. It is easy to get things completely wrong because you can't 'see the forest for the trees'.

Growth does not happen when you are closed-minded. It happens when you are open to gaining new perspectives and learning new ideas. If you listen carefully to your partner's argument there may be part of it that modifies your own thinking. Rather than view conflict as a battleground in which one has to defeat the other, think about what could be gained if both viewpoints were taken into account. They may not be mutually exclusive.

If I have learned one thing through working as a therapist it is that there are always many perspectives to any one situation. It is always fascinating to work with one partner, to accept their view of the world, only to hear a totally different perspective from the other partner. In your relationship conflict, both perspectives of any argument are likely to be valid. If you really take the time to understand the other side of the argument you may be surprised how much it changes your own perspective. At the end of the day, reality is what exists in your own brain. You can change your perspective through broadening your understanding.

I have learned that absolutes rarely exist and that there are many perspectives of what is 'right'. Learn either to step back from a line of argument or 'position' in order to value alternative views, or agree to differ in opinion. So much can be lost if you hold to a passion to be right or the need to be logical and rational.

If there is conflict in your relationship it may be masking fears and insecurities. Ask yourself if you are missing an underlying issue that is hard for you or your partner to express. If your partner is angry with you, remember that there is likely to be some emotional hurt underneath, something he or she finds difficult to express. Anger is, in comparison, an easy outlet. You might be misinterpreting their side of the argument, especially if it seems irrational. You might win the logic argument per se, but will miss what is important to your partner. For instance, if your partner gets hysterical about you going to dance class every Monday night it might seem irrational, but underneath there might be a deep fear that you are going somewhere else, or going to meet someone new. His distress may have nothing to do with the dance class.

Hurt and blame
Regardless of how long you have been together, it is exceedingly sad if you or your partner attempt to destroy each

other through a determination to be the one who is blameless. Bitter and vengeful fighting can develop when there is fear of a relationship breakup. Couples can disempower themselves. They become distanced from each other and then forget what brought them together in the first place.

It is easy to jump to an explanation that the other partner has changed, and that it is all their fault. You are on dangerous ground if you become determined to prove that your partner is the one who has wrecked your relationship. If your partner truly has changed, you might need to ask yourself how you have contributed to that change, or what you have done that has encouraged your partner to change in that way. If they were once very laid back and easy to get along with, then what is it that you might have done to drive them unnaturally away from that behaviour?

It would be sad for you and your partner to make each other thoroughly miserable to the point of heartbreak. Conflict is often a cry for help, a cry to regain the emotional intimacy that has started to elude the relationship. Rather than defend your position, it would be much more productive to acknowledge that a change has occurred, and that it is time to respect your differences and put your energy into seeking a compromise. Your heartbreak needs to be turned into loving acts of kindness if you wish to salvage your relationship. This means being willing to let go of past hurt and looking to the future. Keeping a score of disappointments keeps you both in the past. Respectful behaviour needs to prevail. If there are children involved, remember that they are learning through the role modelling they see from both their parents.

Restoring your relationship in times of crisis
I frequently see young couples who are in crisis. Often they report being very much in love in their early days. Through the focus on raising their babies, they find they have lost the art and the habit of meaningful communication. Swept up in the joys and traumas that babies bring, couples report they seem to have slipped into a life that has become routine and shallow. They say they have lost their sense of 'the two of us'

that used to exist pre-children and they grieve for that time despite cherishing their children.

If you and your partner have retreated to a merely transactional relationship, one in which only the bare minimum of communication takes place, you will first need to restore the sense of 'two' in order to begin emotionally reconnecting. This means taking time out to be just the two of you. Connection has to take the place of any bitter conflict between you, and this will only happen if you have sufficient time alone to create connection. Point scoring or keeping tally of wrongs is not helpful. Connection is unlikely to happen unless both of you are at a point where you are willing to let go of past hurt and look to the future.

If your relationship has deteriorated into daily conflict, my guess is that the nature of the fighting is characterised by metaphorical 'external finger pointing'. This means blaming the other for everything, 'It is all your fault!' It is easy to slip into this attitude, especially if you have a penchant for being right. After all, that is the one perception you truly understand. You feel very secure when you convince yourself that you are right. Be careful! It is so easy to entice yourself into a position of certainty and strong judgement from which you slip into that mode of having to defeat your partner with every argument.

From the opposite perspective, if you self-doubt to the point of losing faith in yourself, you are likely to soak up all the blame and assault your own self-esteem. 'Internal finger pointing' is a process of self-blame; 'It is all my fault!' When you lay judgement on yourself and tell yourself that you are the problem, you are falling into as similar a trap as the external blamer. You are making judgements that are biased and destructive, only this time it is directed internally rather than externally. Neither polarity is helpful. It takes two to create conflict.

If you and your partner get caught into circular arguments about who is right and who is wrong, it is often a sign that one or both of you feels unheard. So intent on argument, it is probable that neither of you is listening to the other, or to your

7. Creating family

own heart. Finger pointing is the antithesis of what is needed in a relationship. You have to listen and be heard, and in a committed relationship it is reasonable to expect that you be emotionally 'held' and cared for by the other, even in times of disagreement.

If you and your partner are having difficulty with your communication, counselling sessions might provide the space you both need to address issues in a safe and respectful way. In these kinds of sessions, each participant is supported to express their concerns and fears. One of the biggest obstacles to the achievement of a positive relationship is the shame that some individuals seem to feel in relation to seeking counselling. People who feel like this seem to also have some kind of shame attached to not being able to sort the conflict on their own. This reflects a lack of understanding about counselling.

Working on your relationship requires courage and humility. What people often don't realise is that, regardless of your level of maturity, there are always aspects of yourself that you don't see. This is also true for couples. A good couple's counsellor will see things beyond your awareness. As an outsider, the counsellor can bring valuable alternative perspectives that will help you focus on what is working well, what is not working well, and what still needs to be improved or changed.

Another fear about going for couple's therapy is the belief that any expression of true feelings will amount to opening a 'can of worms', or 'opening the floodgates'. You might fear that if you criticise your partner a big argument will erupt. This could be a real possibility if finger pointing was allowed to take place during the session. This will not happen with a good couple's counsellor. No one likes to feel judged. The normal response to finger pointing is hostility. A counsellor will help you make a request for change by owning your own feelings around the issue, and expressing concerns from your own experience without blaming the other.

The use of 'I' language forces you to acknowledge your own experience, e.g. 'I am having difficulty with you being away so much'. This is very different to saying something like, 'You are never here!' This last comment is bound to cause the other person to feel criticised, and to react in a hostile way. Hostility breeds hostility. The difference might seem subtle, but the first statement accepts that there may be many reasons for the speaker feeling this way that might have nothing to do with their partner being away.

If you put yourself on the receiving end of a 'you' statement that is judgemental, it is difficult to refrain from going into a defensive mode. When you own a feeling using 'I' language it leaves the door open to express your feelings, even if they are unfair, unjust, politically incorrect, or exaggerated. When you use a 'you' statement, it implies that the other person is responsible for the way you feel and this incites a hostile reaction. If you take the trouble to express what you feel you are less likely to engender an unproductive hostile reaction.

If you express what you truly feel, you might find that your partner will come to appreciate the motivations behind your words. Both your perspectives may change. In the course of two busy lives it is easy for mistakes to be made, and actions to be misread. When placed in context, the understanding of the real situation can look very different. If you choose to jump to negative conclusions about your partner's behaviour, you are looking for reasons to justify your point of view. Before becoming angry and upset, take time out to find out what the real motive was behind the action you perceive to be so awful. It is the motivation that counts most, not what happened.

Markers for success
In my experience, one of the most obvious and basic indicators of whether a relationship will be sustained is the ability of both partners to be able to reflect on their contribution to any conflict. You need to care enough and be honest enough to verbalise what you have done wrong, despite the risk of shame or humiliation. You also need to be willing to 'do' differently in the future, and be willing to effect the necessary changes in your own attitude and actions. You might also need to start by considering how you plan to nurture the other in the future.

7. Creating family

One of the most common attitude issues I see in therapy work is the blame continuum. At one end of the spectrum, people totally blame others when anything goes wrong in their life, and at the other end totally blame themselves when things go wrong. Everyone presents somewhere along that spectrum. While you may be well-balanced when there is no stress, once high stress is imposed you will likely slide down the slippery slide into the behaviour that comes most naturally to you ... down the neural pathway that has been strongly built in the past.

External blamers are easy to spot. 10-year olds will typically claim:

> 'It wasn't me ... I didn't do it!'
>
> 'It is their fault, they made me.'
>
> 'I don't care, it is their problem.'
>
> 'You can't make me ... I'm going to get them, they'll be sorry.'

Then,

> 'Oops! I am in jail!'

Internal blamers are not so easy to spot. If you internally blame, you are likely to torture yourself often with negative private self-talk:

> 'It's all my fault, I stuffed up.'
>
> 'I should have known better.'
>
> 'I should have known that would happen, if only I had ... '
>
> 'I'm hopeless.'
>
> 'I'm useless.'
>
> 'I wish I could just go away.'

> *'I'm depressed.'*

And then,

> *'Life does not feel worth living.'*

Each extreme end of the responsibility spectrum brings dire consequences, where behaviour is unhealthy and socially unacceptable. Clearly the healthy response is where you reflect on your own behaviour and take responsibility for any wrong or any negative part you played in a situation, but where you are also able to be assertive and push back the things that you do not need to take responsibility for. If you each do this there is a way forward, a way to problem-solve and work through your difficulties. Without honesty and apology, ongoing conflict is inevitable.

Sometimes relationships survive under stress where one partner is an external blamer and the other is an internal blamer. This is a nice little circuit that can work really well for a time. He blames, she apologises. I recently observed this dynamic in a couple who had been married 35 years. The wife, who was the internal blamer, had started to 'fight back', and the husband became increasingly unhappy. He didn't see why things needed to change, but she had seen the light. She eventually refused to take on her husband's blame. She refused to be the problem anymore.

Balance is the key. It is easy to remain in a balanced position when your life is smooth. It is not so easy when you are under stress. It is tempting when you are under stress to slip into your favoured and well-practiced responsibility stance, either to self-blame or rush to blame others.

Know honestly what your usual process is. Use strong self-talk to prevent yourself from sliding into a habitual and destructive response. Own whatever it is that you need to own, but also express what you do not need to own. Be fair to yourself and your partner.

Healthy and unhealthy systems

Systems theory suggests that relationships are made up of many small systems: the mother/father, mother/daughter, mother/son, mother/daughter/son, father/son, father/daughter, father/son/daughter, etc. Each of these subsystems operate their own little structure around 'do's and do not's' for that subsystem. When all systems operate and individuals get their needs met within a family, the system works well. When one person 'misses out', a ripple starts to run through the family. Negative feedback breeds negative responses, and the slide is downhill. Negative patterns develop and repeat themselves over and over: e.g. he teases, she gets annoyed, he shouts. She then tantrums and storms off. Neither talk for a week.

It is useful to analyse what happens in your relationship. Once you can identify your habitual patterns of relating, you can choose to change the pattern at any point. This will send ripples of change through the relationship, and the negative spiral will hopefully reverse into an upward trend.

Ordinarily systems are changed when they are observed to be dysfunctional or inefficient. In relationships people are often oblivious to the negative patterns that develop where the same pattern of interaction is repeated over and over. If you can firstly identify the pattern operating, and secondly encourage different behaviour, then you will effect change. Sometimes even the smallest changes bring about ripples that can cause a redirection towards a positive spiral. Suddenly a door opens to the possibility of change, and the belief of impending disaster is suspended long enough for some real change to take place. Sometimes a simple kindness shown to your spouse can start a ripple of change through showing that you care.

Another useful way of looking at your relationship is to identify the differences in any core beliefs that you and your partner hold that affect the relationship negatively. These beliefs are usually entrenched, and may be slightly hidden from immediate awareness. A good couples' therapist will assist you with this, because it is something that is not easy to be aware of on your own. It is a luxury to have the perspective of someone outside the relationship having an impartial view of the negative influences. This process can be enlightening.

It takes a serious commitment to be willing to confront the perspectives of yourself that you hold dear and sacred. The more 'right' you think you are about the way the world is or should be, the more likely it is that your blind spot has substance.

7.2. Violence, anger, possession, and paranoia... power and control

It is so important to recognise behaviours that border on power and control. It can be a very claustrophobic life if someone tries to trap you in an abusive relationship. In these kinds of relationships, the outside world is kept at a wide distance from the internal workings of the family that is ruled by domination and power. In a healthy family, each person is allowed the opportunity to do their growing outside the family environment. This is fundamental to nurturing and sustaining a long-term relationship. In an abusive situation where contact with the outside world is controlled and censored, there is a danger of domination and control escalating to become abuse.

If you experience a lack of trust in your partner to hold you in a safe place, this can lead to a downward spiral in your respect for your partner. There is something wrong if you start to fear your partner. If you begin to develop compulsive behaviours to overcome your fear, your mental health is really at risk. These kinds of fears and obsessions, once developed, can be far reaching through your life if allowed to continue over long periods.

I am reminded of a client whose wife had cheated on him. He then found a relationship that brought him great joy, however, he was so anxious that the new partner would also cheat on him that he asked her upfront not to tell him anything about her past with other men because it would 'play on his mind'. I asked him to take ownership of what he was saying, e.g. 'I allow my mind to play with ideas of her cheating on me ...'

7. Creating family

Taking ownership of his thought process allowed him to change his own attitude. This proved to be a far healthier way of approaching the issue.

I had one lovely client who had escaped an abusive first marriage to find love with a kind and loving man. She developed a significant spending obsession that she explained fed her lingering sense of not being good enough. Another client, an experienced police officer, could not handle being demeaned by the subtle but nasty 'behind the scene' teasing from fellow officers. Just as victims of crime suffer ongoing disempowerment that comes with loss of dignity and personal choice, so to do targets of bullying, domination, and control.

Violent relationships can impact people for life. These kinds of behaviours often develop slowly and gradually progress into behaviours that become dangerous. As one partner becomes more and more controlled by the other, it becomes increasingly difficult to move in and out of the relationship. These relationships are complex in the myriad of emotions they produce and for the targeted partner there is often shock and shame in admitting they have got themselves into this kind of relationship.

If you are caught in this kind of relationship, know that there are many courageous individuals whose footsteps you can follow. These are people from all walks of life who have called a halt to domination and control, and have moved out of poisonous relationships under physical threat, with no assets to their name. While it takes huge courage to make this move, know that there are many who will rally to reach out and help you if you are prepared to seek help.

If you are being abusive towards your partner, know that it will stay with your partner and will forever stand in the way of your partner viewing you with respect. If you are being abused and you are tempted to respond in kind towards your abusive partner, be careful. Know that it will not improve your situation and will not help you feel good about yourself. If you lash out physically or verbally you may put yourself in potential danger.

One client whose wife had just seen an old boyfriend for coffee, felt so angry that he became physically aggressive towards her. After a time he became quite remorseful, but could not understand why his wife would not give him another chance. He thought any behaviour was tolerable as long as there was an apology that went with it. He just did not get it. Abuse is not easily forgotten or forgiven. Think carefully before you judge your partner's behaviour. Use your words to communicate what you feel, and make your request about what you would like them to change. If your partner truly loves you, there is a good chance they will meet your request but you cannot force them to do something just because it is what you want.

Power, control, and the drama void

It is curious that some couples manage to sustain abusive relationships over many years. Constant argument, behaviour that demeans, and 'big drama' often mark these relationships. The constant misery seems predictable and strangely comfortable for the participants. One may well ask what they would be doing if not constantly bickering. How do they avoid intimacy by keeping each other at arm's length with disrespectful behaviour? How do they get away with bullying behaviours?

I recall one client who acknowledged that life would seem boring without relationship dramas. She truly wanted to be able to live peacefully without drama, but at the same time, acknowledged it was like an addiction. As we examined her life, she realised that she needed something to fill the gap left by a husband who worked seven days a week. Being drawn into a drama was welcome relief from her boring weekends alone. Without some drama going on it was as if there was a void in her life that she had an insatiable urge to fill, even if she had to create drama herself.

Another client struggled valiantly to change his deeply held cultural belief that his wife was his possession. He had to learn that any form of control takes people out of mutual relationship and into an aggressive/submissive relationship.

He had stepped over the line and put his rights before hers on many occasions. He had lost her. He had been so consumed by his own hurt (of his own making) that he had assumed the right to hurt his wife.

Getting over the ingrained notion of his wife being his possession was a hurdle he had to jump before anything else made sense. There were many other things he had to learn. He would report that he felt so angry all the time. He had always expressed his anger in violent ways. It was a revelation to him that the emotion under anger is generally hurt. As he learned to express his hurt, his anger dispersed, and his relationships improved. He had to learn assertion skills in order to state his case and ask for what he wanted, instead of demanding it. He had to learn the nature of body language, and above all he had to learn to let things go instead of giving focus to the need to control everything.

8

The sensing child

8.1. Learning from children

8.2. The art of parenting

8.3. The difference between tough love and abuse

8.4. Children learning from parents and extended family

8.5. Difficult times

8.1. Learning from children

If you are a new parent and you really feel like you don't know what you are doing, take relief from the fact that most parents feel this way the first time around. It is definitely a 'learn on the job' situation. If you have really strong ideas about what you will and will not do, you will probably find you will have to let go of a lot of those preconceived notions. Your baby is expert in his or her needs, and will signal what is needed. They don't have words, so they rely on other cues. You will soon learn the different types of cry that your baby uses to tell you what is wrong. They are all different, and no one regime fits everything. You will find it is often trial and error 'til you hit the jackpot and finally see a continuing look of contentment.

Every day your child is building new neural pathways, making connections, learning patterns, and starting to get a notion of how to communicate with you. They learn through hearing the patterns of the language. They love repetitive rhymes because they can start to make some sense of what they hear. They start to anticipate certain actions as you sing to them. Children rely on their senses to absorb the world around them. Where a child will actively seek out experiences that involve all their senses, adults often lose the ability to interpret the data that all their senses bring. Adults narrow their focus to things they rely on in order to be functional in a hectic world.

Babies and toddlers love exploring their world. You don't have to provide all the latest play equipment – an eight-month old is just as happy with a wooden spoon as a sophisticated toy. Everything is so new to them that they ooze with joy and delight when they see something unexpected. Primary school children also look eagerly for newness and fun. Have you ever really watched a young child explore their world? I love to watch an 18-month old child gallop courageously toward a hazard, then look up to read the expression on their mother's face. His or her little world takes shape continually with each step into the unknown. Without the wisdom of experience there are inevitable crashes. You can't protect them from all these crashes, only minimise the chance of really serious ones.

It is curious that children learn so much and yet seem to lose so much from their conscious memory, remembering some things but not others. A first ride on an elephant at the zoo might be forgotten, whereas the memory of their brother's expression when he accidentally dropped their ice cream into the monkey's cage can remain as vivid as if it happened yesterday. A child's whole personality is built through layer upon layer of experiences, both good and bad, boring or funny, sad or happy. It is interesting the way children use their senses far more than adults. They 'really' smell things, they 'really' hear things. They love touching different textures, and they are often quite adamant about the tastes they like and don't like. The world is full of visual excitement; a tiny ant climbing a mound of earth, a firetruck zooming up the road. Adults can

8. The sensing child

learn a great deal from children about staying in touch with their senses.

Children form strong attachments to the things that bring them comfort within the world they understand. There is not only attachment to their parents; there may also be attachment to a particular toy, a teddy bear, their mother's dressing gown, or another adult. Adults remember the things that are out of the ordinary, and they remember the way they felt when they engaged in a particular activity. A sense of fun stays forever, as does the sense of achievement that comes with mastery of a new skill. Special moments like the first solo bike ride or the first footy goal have significance and become a part of instant recall.

Sometimes there are exciting memories of times that were a little risky. Children thrive on excitement and risk-taking, especially when they have a stable emotional base. It is your job as a parent to provide this stable emotional base. It is easy to pick the children who lack a stable emotional base. They are fearful of whatever will happen next in their lives. They go home from school feeling anxious and with resignation to survive another day. They seem uneasy and often have a feeling of being trapped and unable to change anything.

Children gradually form their own ideas about what is right and what is wrong. They see and discern dishonesty, weakness, selfishness, and hypocrisy. Children may be unable to verbalise what they think and feel, but they have a consciousness that shapes their being and their choices. It may seem that your child is too little to know anything, and yet young children often have an amazing ability to call situations with stark simplicity. Their truth can be painful as they utter things like:

> 'You never listen to me'

> 'Aunty [X] only comes here to talk to you, so why do I have to be here?'

> 'Mum goes crook at us for hitting each other, and then she hits us to teach us a lesson'.

Your children probably understand a lot more than you give them credit for. When you really listen to young children they can be very astute in what they observe and say.

Children also enjoy testing the limits of their own power, independence, and security. They thrive on making their own decisions. Suitable risk helps them grow and learn. They constantly explore and push the boundary of what they are allowed to do. If you have a child with a strong, determined personality, it can be frustrating at times. They often want to call their own shots and do their own thing with only childish knowledge of what they need. It is so easy to interpret this desire for self-determination as naughty behaviour, or initiative gone astray, but the more intelligent and spirited the child, the more they will be determined to master their world.

This is a good thing for your child in the long run. As a parent you just have to wear the frustration, knowing that you have an intelligent and strong-minded young person who will take charge of their world. The way you handle this strength will be according to the parenting style you adopt so it is worth giving thought to the kind of parenting style you intend to follow. Read widely and acquire tips from experienced parents around you.

8.2. The art of parenting

Building good self-esteem is the key to good parenting

Good self-esteem is the key to growing happy children who are emotionally healthy and strong. It is not helpful for you to give your children constant praise. If you are constantly praising your child there can be no space for them to experience and savour their own success. With false praise the child is likely to find themselves in a strange space where they feel they don't measure up to the praise their parents give them. Allow them space to feel their own success and build their own self-esteem.

8. The sensing child

I have not come across any normal, healthy children with high self-esteem who have severe behavioural problems. When family environments are such that everyone's needs are cared for, where everyone is 'held' emotionally, then positive patterns of interaction develop. Self-esteem is well developed. Conversely, when needs are not met and self-esteem is assaulted, the downward spiral develops and continues to descend until there is some kind of crisis. Sometimes the crisis can spark a resurgence of loving intentions that have previously been buried in issues of frustration and control.

At other times, when adults command control at any cost and use judgemental comments that demean or make the child feel badly about themselves, the spiral heads downwards. Similarly, when adults use physical strength to overpower or control a child they render the child powerless. Different personalities deal with things in different ways. The child may withdraw and be prone to being a victim, or they may hold resentment that is likely to erupt later during adolescence into ingrained conflict. They may lash out even more. In the heat of the moment, parents often forget to apply consequences, and instead lash out verbally or physically.

Regardless of the quality of family life, the family is like a stage from which you see the world. If you stand on stage and look out with confidence you will see a lot more than if you stand self-absorbed in your own anxiety, battling with your low self-esteem. Your children need to feel loved and confident in finding their own way.

If your children have grit, they will survive all kinds of life difficulties. For this they need to have an attitude that delights in opportunities for growth of any kind. Rather than praising achievements or intelligence, it is important to praise effort and perseverance. Above all, your response to failure is extremely important. If failure is shaming, your child will prefer to opt out than go through that again. No one likes to feel shame. If failure is celebrated for effort and perseverance, and seen as an opportunity for growth, then there is no shame – only more work to be done.

The art of parenting is about knowing when and how to encourage and empower, and knowing when and how to limit the elastic rope of independence in a way that is firm, respectful, and nurturing. Once you enter into a power struggle with your child, you have lost. While children can be out of control and have no insight into their own behaviour, they remember what their parent said to them in the heat of the moment – it sticks! So many times have I had young people in my office telling me all the inappropriate things said to them by their much loved father or mother.

It seems particularly common that fathers feel the need to 'stay on top' and be the dominant male who keeps the family members under control. They seem to have high expectations, particularly with first-born sons. The fear of losing control seems to push these dads to a position where they feel they have to be a strong authority figure who has the power and position to praise or put down the children, according to their own needs at the time. Unfortunately, the relationship becomes about the father, not about the child.

The trouble is when you make a child feel bad about themselves through harsh or demeaning accusation you shatter their self-esteem. This is a feeling that stays with them for life. They are moments of truth that do not fade away. The feeling is embedded in the child's psyche, a feeling of being unworthy. So much adult therapy involves trying to restore really deep feelings of low self-esteem.

Moments of truth stand out for children. They are stark and sharp, and leave a footprint on their soul. It only takes 30 seconds to say something that hurts, insults, or demeans a child. Negative expectation is contagious. When children are trying to do better, but still find themselves the subject of constant negative expectation, it becomes too hard. Eventually they live up to the negativity that has been thrown at them. They go out of their way to engage in self-harming behaviours of one kind or another. It is so sad to see and so hard to change, because the hurts are deeply embedded in a past that is often beyond memory. Yet, moments of truth may also be positive.

8. The sensing child

Children remember fun and times of gaiety. The little quips that parents and grandparents make can stay etched in the brain, to be laughed about years later.

Many adults are really uncomfortable with expressing their emotion in any context. When children come into the world most parents soften and gain some maternal or paternal feelings. Others have bottled-up feelings that just don't come out easily. If this is you, be honest and upfront about it. The most powerful thing you can do for your child is to let them know that you are the one who has difficulty in this area. Tell them that you find it hard to say how you feel, but you want to encourage them to talk about their feelings. Tell them that you love and admire them but don't often feel comfortable showing it. Children understand more than you think. If you are big enough to give them this explanation you will probably release them from years of distress thinking they are the ones at fault, that something about them stops you from connecting with them and showing them love. It will save them thinking that they are unlovable. Think about it from your child's perspective.

Be mindful about the similarities and differences within the family. If you have all but one person in the family who lives in their head, how does that one person connect with others? A highly emotional child in a highly cognitive family will suffer. Alternatively a highly cognitive child in a highly emotional family will also suffer. It is a lonely place for a child who seems to understand the world very differently from everyone else in the family.

Understanding normal development
Children naturally see the world in relation to themselves. This is not selfishness, it is developmentally normal behaviour. To understand another person's perspective is a sophisticated concept and takes careful explanation that is developmentally appropriate. Children generally find it hard to cope with abstract ideas until well into their teenage years. It is hard for them to imagine how someone else might feel. They first have to

know how they would feel themselves in a similar circumstance which could be very difficult if such a circumstance is beyond their experience.

This is not to say that empathy training is useless. It is always helpful, as long as it is not accompanied with any hidden messages telling the kids they are bad. It needs to include a positive explanation of how to behave in the future. The art of parenting is to love, nurture, and support children to believe in themselves. Don't expect kids to know the right thing to do in new circumstances; spell it out to them. Explain why they need to do certain things. Tell them what will be expected of them when they attend a family BBQ.

For families to stay connected as each member grows and develops, it is great to eat meals together, or at least the evening meal. Your children cannot be allowed to dominate the family through tantrums, aggression, talking back, or whining. Your discipline needs to be consistent and fair with short-term consequences that are inconvenient, rather than arduous. Simply remove them until they are ready to behave appropriately. Poor behaviour needs to be responded to straight away. Children need to understand that they may always make a request, and that the request may be granted on some occasions, and not on others. Make sure your delivery of this message is respectful. It is unfair to quash your child's expression of what they want or need. It is never okay to shame or ridicule a child. Children naturally learn through making mistakes. If they are ridiculed they will withdraw from taking the risk. Children need to make mistakes. It is one way they learn limits and consequences. They need to be nurtured, guided with firm limits, and encouraged to take safe risks.

When your child does something wrong
We often think children should know how to behave. Rather than berate the child, address the behaviour and educate your child about why it should not be repeated. Think carefully when you are taking your child into a new situation or new experience, and explain what will be required of them in advance.

Rather than give into demands, listen to their requests. Explain the situation, and ask what the child thinks should happen. Rather than bribe, set fair and reasonable limits. Enforce rules consistently, or you will teach your child how to manipulate you. Respect your child's need for independence and the need to control their own safe space. Remember, as much as you would like it, your baby can't stay your baby forever.

Routines can get fragmented, and there will be times when there seems to be little order in the house. Rather than take it out on the kids by screaming orders at them, call the household together and explain the situation. Seek their assistance to put the house back in order. Identify something nice that will happen when the order is restored.

Fear teaches children to be dishonest
If children fear your reaction to the truth they are more likely to lie and be secretive. They will fear the overreaction that they think will eventuate. If you realise you have been a little 'over the top' or harsh, sit down with your child and make a plan for changing the behaviour. If the lies are severe and the child is approaching adolescence, it might be necessary to demonstrate how seriously you feel about the truth that you temporarily decide to put aside a consequence as long as they are absolutely honest with you. This is a way of making them take notice of how important it is that they tell you the truth. It is not something to repeat, it is simply a demonstration of how important it is to be honest. You only use this strategy when you feel you have to go back to square one to teach your teen the habit of being truthful. Reintroduce consequences once the child is well practiced in the art of truth-telling.

Overprotection is disempowering
If you are a helicopter parent who hovers over your children to protect them in all circumstances, you are denying them the experience of making their own decisions. This will cause your child to lose confidence in their capacity to make decisions and to avoid taking risks of any kind. Loss of self-esteem will

likely follow as your child becomes diffident about every aspect of growing up. Stand back, empower your children to make their own decisions. Trust them to make good choices. Show them you have faith in them and understand that any error of judgement on their part is just a learning glitch.

Maladaptive behaviours children use to get their needs met

Children who are constantly angry continue this behaviour because they get something out of it. They are assured of negative attention, and they feel this is better than no attention. The solution is obvious. Ignore poor behaviour and acknowledge good behaviour, and the cycle of anger and frustration will subside. Remember, it is better for children to get attention from positive behaviour than have to resort to negative behaviour that brings more and more attention to perpetuate the behaviour. Children who intentionally annoy others generally lack positive attention.

If children have poor self-esteem they need encouragement and support to overcome their self-doubt. What they don't need is harsh judgement, control, or constant direction. If they are told constantly how they should be, they lose their capacity to be self-directed. They also get the message that their feelings don't matter, and they are likely to treat other people that way. Praise and discipline needs to happen in private if there are other children around. Being humiliated or put on a pedestal does the child no favours.

Children learn more from how you say things than from what you say. Arrogance breeds arrogance. Belligerence breeds belligerence. If you are short-tempered, it is likely your child will be, too. If you are negative about yourself, your child will learn that is the way to think about yourself. Yes, it is scary! They learn so much from you every day of their lives. By the time they are 12 they know everything about you. They know your values and beliefs, your inconsistencies, your weaknesses, and your strengths. They know more about you than you know about yourself. If they want a point of rebellion they will easily find it in the very area you hold most dear.

8. The sensing child

If your child is shy
Take notice of your child's personality. Is your child introverted or extraverted, inhibited or shy? Every aspect of personality has its good points and bad points. If your child is quite shy, help them take small steps to build their confidence. Expose them to lots of environments where they are encouraged to interact with new people. Coax them into waving goodbye or hello. Rather than label them as shy, tense, or aggressive in front of other people, keep your observations to yourself. They are not helpful. Simply support and encourage your child in relaxed atmospheres.

Without pressure, your child will gradually take on new challenges. Going into a shop to buy something can be a huge challenge for some kids. Light-hearted persistence and gradual exposure to such an interaction will ease your child into the behaviour. Making a big thing out of it can make your child dig their heels in. I have seen young men in their 20s who struggle with anxiety when they want to go and buy a burger. Work on this while your child is younger. Help them push through the anxieties they experience and encourage them to feel proud of their successes.

8.3. The difference between tough love and abuse

There is nothing wrong with being firm with your child. I am convinced that they feel more secure when they know the limits. It is inconsistency that puts kids in an anxious and insecure place. With adolescents, tough love is sometimes necessary when adolescents fail to learn how to take responsibility for their actions. Tough love applies expected and realistic consequences. When it is accompanied by respect, there is validation for good effort and attitude. The boosts to self-esteem and confidence are what justify the tough love.

Of course, kids learn to manipulate their parents when they know that [X] behaviour produces [Y] results, however, they are also quick to learn from consistent consequences.

Inconsistency is an open invitation for the child to try it on, just in case you say yes.

Emotional abuse is when you criticise a person rather than their behaviour, perhaps using a derogatory term to label them as bad in some way. Physical and sexual abuse is easy to identify. We know when someone steps over the line physically, and sexually. Emotional abuse is sometimes tricky to identify, especially if it is very subtle. Fleeting moments that are quickly healed and repaired may be described as hurts. Those moments are forgotten because they were not intentional and they don't keep happening.

A particularly demeaning comment from someone you love and respect may be much more than a fleeting hurt. It may stay forever. Similarly, hurt that stays with you because it is repeated over and over, or has a nasty edge to it, is emotional abuse. Like bullying, the repeated nature of abuse has a long-term impact. Positives are clouded by this kind of hurt. Therapy rooms are filled with people trying to recover from the emotional abuse they experienced as a child.

Educate rather than chastise
When comments and chastisements are inconsistent, the problem is a lot more serious, especially if the child has not set out to be mean, selfish, or naughty. Children know when they are doing the wrong thing. To be chastised when they haven't meant to do anything wrong can do a lot more damage. The child feels misunderstood and very bad about themselves. The critical thing here is that they feel bad about their past behaviour, and their hurt emotion clouds the possibility of learning better behaviour. For instance, a child who rushes in front of the family to get first in the line for ice cream is just being a normal, self-centred kid. The child does not set out to be rude or aggressive in their movement. They are just thinking of getting the ice cream quickly and don't understand that this is bad behaviour. A gentle, 'It is good manners to stand back and take your turn', or, 'I would like you to move back and let the lady beside you have her turn' are respectful and instructive

comments, whereas a harsh rebuke labels the child as selfish and rude. This kind of comment diminishes and demeans the child whose takeaway message is that they are 'bad'.

If you express judgemental comments coming from a need to keep the child in their place, the child begins to fear opening their mouth to say anything. They lose their spontaneity and start to mutter under their breath, dreading that if they say what they think they will get emotionally slammed. Eventually this can result in deeply held resentment to a parent who seems to not have their best interests in mind. If it keeps happening, children start to accept snide comments as normal. This is an even bigger concern.

Children in emotionally, physically, or sexually abusive families will often believe the abusive behaviours to be normal. They can go into shock when told by an outsider that the behaviour they are experiencing constitutes abuse. Children accept their life as the norm until they see enough of other lives to learn that their own is different. Young adults commonly report to me that they had no idea that their family was strange or different until they were old enough to draw comparisons with their friends.

What is learned in childhood carries into adult life
If you reflect on childhood memories it will be the peaks and troughs that come to mind. The moments of truth, both good and bad, replay in your memory over and over. The feelings can sweep over you, producing over the top emotions that might be joyous or terrifying. Therapy is often about learning to deal with the behaviours that seem to come out of nowhere. Remember, our memories are closely linked to our senses. A smell or sight can send you down the slippery slide to a past occasion where you experienced the same set of emotions in a traumatic situation. Before you know it, you might be acting like the five-year-old who was made to feel shame for taking a cookie from the jar. When the memories are traumatic, the slippery slide is quick and steep and can catch you off guard. The memories can be painful and difficult to deal with.

8.4. Children learning from parents and extended family

Relatives, grandparents and parents provide children with a deep sense of the family as an important part of a bigger world. There is intergenerational learning that moulds attitudes, values, and behaviours in ways that are very subtle. When this influence is positive, the ripple effects of good self-esteem propel young people towards success.

When the influence is negative, it can take years in therapy to remove the dysfunctional feelings of low self-worth. What you learn as children you can pass on unwittingly to the next generation unless you reassess your parenting style and attitude to children. As an adult you role model the way to deal with the world through body language, attitude, reactions to hostile situations, etc. What you role model is incredibly powerful because children absorb it without realising it.

Role modelling starts from birth. Young babies engage in communication long before they can see or talk. They constantly observe and make sense of their world. They learn to get their needs met, whether it be through crying, smiling, squirming, or staging a tantrum. When a child is rude or is lashing out physically or verbally, know that their behaviour is probably learned from someone close to them.

When adult relationships break down

What is not so obvious is something that comes up countless times when talking with parents about their children, especially around times of parental separation. Too often I have heard accounts of terrible rows between parents and step-parents, told through the eyes of tearful children who have been traumatised by the experience. When children can't trust how adults will treat each other, they become anxious and insecure. If they experience inconsistency in the way each parent treats them, they become insecure. When they are confused by double messages, this can put them at risk of severe mental health issues further down the track.

As I mentioned earlier, our adult view of the world is built by experiences that are imprinted on our memory, layer upon layer, from birth. Constant violent or serious conflict in front of children not only induces anxiety and insecurity, it creates a norm for relationship behaviour.

It provides a very poor blueprint for how relationships are managed, one that may perpetuate dysfunctional communication down to subsequent generations in ways you might never imagine. If you are in this situation, think carefully about how you wish to conduct yourself, and how you wish to be seen in the eyes of your children. Keep adult conflict between the adults.

Children cope better with facts than fantasy
Life is never perfect. People are never perfect. I have not been, nor met, the perfect parent. Parents do the best they can with what they know at the time. Children often sense when something is amiss. When big things happen, I often hear parents say, 'Oh, he is too young to understand'. Sensing without knowing is a frightening experience. A sense of foreboding can be worse than knowing the facts.

It is easy to make the mistake of not explaining 'adult things' to kids because your own mind is filled with complexity. For kids, life can be made simpler with a few facts.

Once they have the facts, they are often surprisingly capable of adapting to any new situation. When simple truths are denied, children create their own fantasy around what they think is happening. Fantasy can terrify them.

8.5. Difficult times
Children are very accepting and matter of fact about all kinds of things, even their own terminal illness. Clients have told me how special it is to see the world through the eyes of their sick child. Where the parents bring complex understandings,

children cut through complexity and accept the unacceptable. Children are often very astute about what is not being said, even if they don't have words to describe their feelings. When parents shy away from the facts in order to protect their own fears, the child senses the fear and often develops some kind of insecurity or need that invariably goes unmet.

Children can be incredibly resourceful. I remember one young 12-year-old boy who was the prime carer for his disabled father. He accepted what he had to do physically, but what he could not cope with was his father's unpredictable discipline, and what seemed to him to amount to emotional blackmail. The son was expected to be a child when the father was feeling on top of things, and to be the parent when the father was not coping with his disability. One minute the boy had to be an adult and the next minute a boy again.

In situations like this, children can develop adult maturity because they are frequently called upon to function as an adult. It is sad enough when adult responsibilities are thrust upon children through some tragic circumstance. It is incredibly sad when parents expect their young child to have adult sensibilities because it is important for the adult that their child is seen as highly intelligent, or even worse, a 'genius'. I have known adults who expect their children to be little adults. While children need age-appropriate facts, they also need life to be full of innocence and joy, rather than regimented knowledge acquisition and adult expectations

I recently saw a client who had been a victim of abuse as a child. He had built a good life for himself through his sheer determination to succeed, however, his terrible outbursts of anger at home greatly distressed his family, which included teenagers. His response to them was that their life was 100 times better than his own, so why should they complain? He rationalised to himself that he need not have any sympathy for their distress. He had come to accept his upbringing as the norm, and therefore his kids were having it better than he did. Sadly, he was destroying all he had worked so hard to achieve. So often this is the case. It is so easy to come to accept our experience as the norm and fail to evaluate, and see beyond it. This man was risking losing his precious family unless he could acknowledge his own bad experience and make a fundamental shift to wanting something better for his children.

Of course, some may say that kids should not be protected from the real world of conflict and harsh realities. My response to this is that children live what they see. Children are more likely to lead happy lives if they learn good anger management and conflict resolution skills at home. There is every chance that their life will be far happier than the children of families who present with ongoing trauma and conflict. As one of my clients said, 'I grew up in a family with ongoing drama. I know I don't have to get involved in our family dramas, but I'm kind of used to it and life seems boring if there is no drama going on'.

It is much easier to learn good skills from the beginning than to retrieve bad habits, whether it be anger management or smoking, because it takes perseverance and support to break through old patterns of behaviour. It also takes a great deal of courage and humility to address attitudinal or communication dysfunction in order to prevent passing on bad habits to the next generation, and the generations that follow. It is worth trying to at least own your mistakes with the awareness that you can have a hugely positive influence on future generations just through role modelling appropriate behaviours when children are young.

9

Understanding adolescents

> 9.1. *The developmental nature of adolescence*
> 9.2. *Supporting adolescents*
> 9.3. *Dealing with difficult behaviour and difficult times*

9.1. The developmental nature of adolescence

Developmental needs

The transformation to adolescence happens very quickly, and it is easy to view it as a problematic and stressful period for the whole family. Many young people grow through adolescence with very few difficulties. They have high confidence, high self-esteem, and seem to understand instinctively what they need to achieve to become an adult.

Parents know rationally that the transformation from child to adult must come, that the young child they have carefully nurtured must grow to become an adult, one they hope will embody all their hopes and dreams. Parents will often ask what they are doing wrong when their teenager makes mistakes. The reality is that adolescents navigate their own pathway through this difficult period. They test the limits physically, and mentally, and emotionally. They know intuitively that they have to 'do for themselves'.

Ideally, they learn to:

- think for themselves
- develop their own unique identity
- establish and maintain mature relationships, including sexual relationships
- gain job skills and future earning capacity, or chosen mission
- develop optimistic and realistic goals for their future
- develop a philosophy and belief set that will underpin the way they will interact with the world.

As adolescents test the boundaries it is wise if you and your partner can agree ahead of time on the kinds of freedoms and the pathways that might be appropriate. If you don't give thought to this you may find that your adolescent is playing you off against each other, capitalising on the different ideas you each hold.

When you have developed a plan in your own mind, share this with your adolescent because he or she is probably thinking they will never be allowed to stay out at a party 'til midnight. Because a particular freedom is not allowed now, they feel total frustration because they think the rule will stand forever. Explain the concept of total freedom at 18 when they become legally free to make their own way. Explain that you will gradually extend the limits in a way that helps them be ready to take that freedom in a mature way.

Adolescents experience a single yearning for freedom with somewhat cloudy specifics. They don't understand that the progression to freedom brings with it responsibility. They don't understand the growing sense of responsibility that needs to be developed concurrently with freedom. They seem to catch the shiny glint of independence that naturally draws them like a magnet. The yearning is often so strong and compelling that adolescents find very creative and often very effective ways

9. Understanding adolescents

to get full freedom straight away. It matters not to them that the means may be inappropriate, or less than ideal by their parents' standards.

They know they must leave childhood behind, and the broad concept of independence becomes the flag they fly as they forge ahead. They equate restriction with a need to rebel. When they resort to inappropriate means, what they usually neglect to see is the impact of their risk taking on their own self-esteem and respect in the eyes of their parents. It really does help if they understand that freedom comes with responsibility, that they are being prepared for full freedom by the time they are 18.

In our wisdom as adults we understand this notion that responsibility accompanies and gives rise to true independence, but it is rarely articulated to young adults. They think they know everything, but they often know little about what it means to be responsible. They have a desperate need to assess and critique the world solely through their own eyes. It is not wise to take their criticism or contrary views too personally. It is a necessary function of their growing up that they critique the world in general, forming their own opinions as they do so.

It is important to acknowledge here that adolescents are often essentially egocentric. It is common for them to see everything from their own viewpoint because that is where they are developmentally. Their brain has not grown to the point of fully understanding empathy. The brain does not completely develop until around 25 years of age. Adolescents have only minimal glimpses of what it is like to be in your shoes, so refrain from calling them selfish or shaming them. By all means point out how their actions are impacting on other members of the family, but know that they probably won't listen. If you point out what impact their behaviour is having on themselves, then you may get their attention. This is normal. As adolescents grow and mature, they gain greater understanding of the world beyond themselves. It happens naturally.

Adolescents may push you away in a bid to become independent. They may become argumentative and difficult to get along with, but you would have far bigger problems if your adolescent was too frightened to go anywhere or too withdrawn to gain any kind of independence.

The pushing away is usually a temporary state. Your parenting career has been aimed at bringing up your child to be independently functioning in the world. Their push for independence is a job well done on your part. Try not to take their criticism personally when they push you away. It is their way of showing you that they are their own person.

Stay strong and confident in the knowledge that if their world crashes for whatever reason, it will be you they will turn to. As they grow and move into the world, their critical stance often proves painful in the long run as they confront the limits of their ability to change or influence the world. As they start to form their own family, their appreciation of what you have done for them will deepen. Hang in there!

9.2. Supporting adolescents

Avoiding self-blame
It seems to be a natural response for parents to blame themselves when their teenager does something undesirable. Parents cringe at inappropriate or illegal adolescent behaviour, and sometimes see it as a reflection of their own parenting. I have even known parents to go a further step and begin to feel sorry for their young adult because they have had such ineffectual parenting. Where does this end? I know of one lady in her 90s who was still blaming herself for her 63-year old daughter's poor behaviour!

I understand that as a parent you might find it hard to take off your protective parenting hat. The trouble is that this attitude distracts you from the task of ensuring that your young person takes responsibility for their own behaviour. By the age of 12, your adolescent knows your values inside-out. They will choose to follow your values or develop their own new set of

9. Understanding adolescents

values. Blaming yourself for creating this problem teenager is a time-waster, and it buys directly into the adolescent's desire to blame you rather than take responsibility for his or her own actions.

It is more productive to look at what your adolescent is gaining by their behaviour. Even though the behaviour might be problematic, you will find that they are gaining something from it. If you can work this out you are on the way to using a whole range of strategies that will help. It could be a sense of belonging (with the wrong crowd), enhanced self-esteem (maybe lying better than their friends), or a behaviour they believe to be cool. If you can identify what they are looking for you can then look constructively for ways to fill that need in a more productive and acceptable manner.

When adolescents have strong self-esteem they are more likely to be able to be their own person, and to find appropriate ways to express that. When self-esteem is low, adolescents are more likely to withdraw and rush to grasp what they need, regardless of how inappropriate it may be.

If it is belonging they crave, then it is better to belong in the wrong group than to feel excluded from the right group. For a child seeking identity and acknowledgement of their importance, the greater the conflict with adults, the more the adolescent sees themselves as their own person rather than a mere reflection of their parents.

When adolescents lack a sense of personal power, they sometimes seek it through rebellion and unreasonable responses to discipline. Sometimes conflict with adults is interpreted as growing independence, but this can backfire when they reject the advice or criticism they need. They can present as aggressive or passive aggressive, determined to gain a sense of power at all costs. With all these behaviours, the stronger the character of the child, the stronger the tug of war with parents.

Staying calm with less overreaction and using natural consequences

Adolescents test their boundaries by trying to manipulate parents to get what they want. This is not about you, it is about your adolescent struggling to find productive ways of getting their perceived needs met.

Arguing with you is a way of affirming to themselves their own identity and independence of thought. If you react or lose control it gives them a false sense of power. The greatest mistake is to take this personally and chastise yourself for producing this wild and snarly individual who bears no resemblance to the sweet child who used to exist two months ago.

Parents need to stay strong and see this striving for power as the adolescent's own difficulty in managing their transition into adulthood. Lectures and lengthy explanations by you are a waste of time. What is required in this situation is for you to shelve your emotional reactions and demonstrate concern for what the adolescent is doing to himself or herself. If you shelve the shock, self-blame, frustration, and all the other kinds of emotional distress that are likely to confront you, you can shift the responsibility to the young person. When you react and become distressed, you make it your problem. Adolescents will rationalise that you, his parents, are so upset, and that means he or she does not need to worry about it.

If you can possibly stay cool, calm, and collected, respond with something along the lines of, 'Gosh, you have got yourself into a tight spot', or, 'Oh! What are you going to do about that?', or, 'Gee, you are not going to like the result of that!'

Whatever you say, frame the discussion by pointing out gently that this is their problem to work out. In doing this you buy out of the problem, leaving responsibility resting squarely on your adolescent's shoulders. If you get hysterical and launch into a lecture, your teenager will see it as your problem, not theirs; after all, you are the one who is upset!

Having faith in your adolescent's ability to get it right

Ultimately, your adolescent may arrive at similar beliefs and behaviours as your own, but what is important for them is that the journey has been one of their own making. This is actually healthy! Hopefully their learning does not result in any major trauma! It is a tricky time for everyone.

It is a time when adults need to be reminded that their child has a full appreciation of their parents' values, beliefs, and feelings. In my experience, adolescents do not generally set out to disappoint or hurt their parents. They are merely seeking to do their growing up in their own way. When there is a crisis or some out of control behaviour, the greatest predictor of future success is whether the young person believes their parent has full faith in them. Your teenager needs to see, hear, and feel that faith. If you don't have faith in their ability to eventually get things right, how can they possibly have any confidence or belief in their own ability to sort things out in the end?

If you belittle, demean, or use negative phrases like, 'You can never get it right', or, 'You are such a dead loss', this will likely become embedded in your adolescent's psyche. You might think they do not listen to anything you say, but they hear every word. Constant criticism of their person is likely to produce entrenched low self-esteem, feelings of inadequacy, and worthlessness. These can last a lifetime! They present time after time in therapy rooms.

Dealing with adolescent behaviour is rarely easy. It is important to stay calm and reasonable, even though this takes considerable effort. It would be very easy to swing into, 'What I say, goes', mode. Some parents make the mistake of taking such a severe approach that their adolescent has no room to move at all. It never surprised me when parents with harsh parenting practices appeared in my office because their daughter had run away and was refusing to come home. Very often it is the failure of the parent to acknowledge that their child is no longer their 'little' girl or boy, nor are they adults. It is understandable that for some this in-between time is like quicksand, where it is hard for either adult or adolescent to gain a strong footing.

When children don't get their needs met they invariably 'act out' in the hope of relieving the discomfort, pain, or confusion they feel. It does not pay to jump to conclusions about what is troubling them. Having the luxury of sitting with a young person and talking to them in depth, I have often found that there are far less obvious reasons for their over the top behaviour. For instance, it is not uncommon to discover that a young person has a strong subconscious drive to bring help to their family, to get Mum and Dad communicating, even if only about their troublesome child.

When there is a crisis, in an adolescent's mind it doesn't matter what happens, as long as something changes because the pain or confusion can't be tolerated any longer. It can be a feeling of being unloved, or something to do with the pain of hearing their parents fight or demean each other. It has always been interesting to observe that when parental issues resolve, there is a miraculous improvement in their adolescent's behaviour.

Adolescents respond well when someone is truly interested in their welfare, their interests, sports, friends, and ideas. What they want most is for their parents to see them as they are, their own person. They want their parents to see that they are no longer the young child who had to accept everything their parent said. They want to be treated like an adult, and the essence of this is not usually about freedom, but about respect. They want you to respect them as the person they are coming to be.

Encourage a sense of purpose in your teenager by talking with them about some realistic goals that they might aim for. Show you have faith and confidence in his or her ability to achieve. Feelings of competence are nurtured in the little things in life through positive feedback. It is the little things you say that engender a sense of importance and significance. Help them feel a sense of belonging in the family and let them know by your actions that they are a valued member. Try to show confidence in their ability to make wise decisions.

Look after your adolescent's self-esteem by showing them respect and ongoing trust that they have the resources to work things out. Talk to them about how you can help them. Ask them about the areas they would like assistance in, then empower them to manage it on their own, rather than take over from them. Families need to show they care, not just in words, but in actions and time.

9.3. Dealing with difficult behaviour and difficult times

As your children grow into adolescents, it seems trickier to deal with their bad behaviour than when they were little. They grow beyond the time where you can send them to their room for time out. Adolescents will often be adamant that they are in the right.

Rather than send your adolescent away because you have had enough, tell them to cool off and that you will talk with them when they have calmed down. Let a little time pass and take them aside. Ask them to talk about why they feel so deeply about the issue, gently pointing out the other points of view they need to take into account. Explain the repercussions for them that they might not have thought of.

If your adolescent's behaviour is rude and aggressive, be quite frank and tell them the specific behaviours that are unacceptable. Ask them to join with you in finding the solution. Be specific, make a short list, and try to work together to achieve a better outcome. Ask what they want to be different and problem-solve together how this might be achieved.

No matter how bolshy or outspoken they are, most adolescents have significant confidence issues at one time or another. They are often confused about where they will fit into the world, and can doubt their ability to sustain a serious relationship, or to be loved. The more they push their family away, the more they are likely to be in need of some serious loving.

Passive aggressive behaviour
Passive aggressive behaviour is very frustrating and tiring. It occurs when children pretend not to care about consequences, or withdraw and simply do nothing in preference to acting out, using backchat, or defiance. Some children learn very early on that if they buy out of being hurt by consequences then their parents or teachers will feel helpless and give up on them. They win! And yet, a child who is behaving in a passive aggressive way has no confidence in their ability to change anything.

This is a sophisticated form of rebellion. It is so important not to buy into this response by giving up. Respond with something like, 'That's interesting that you don't care. Be careful, though: the consequences will keep getting bigger until you start to care'.

Be creative in the way you deal with the issues, and nip this behaviour in the bud as early as possible. When it becomes entrenched, it is really hard to shift. If you see one sign of them giving up the 'I don't care' stance, celebrate their behaviour as a wise choice and show them respect.

Refusal to take responsibility for their actions
If your adolescent evades taking responsibility for their behaviour, understand that they are struggling to grow up. It is time to reassess how harsh you are with your judgements and whether you have been assaulting your adolescent's self-esteem through shaming.

If the application of consequences is not working, it is time to start asking them what they think, about anything! Engage them in adult discussions. Boost their self-esteem and encourage them to take on new interests. Tell them you really need their assistance with something that is real. Take them camping, rely on their strength. Trust their judgement on a bushwalk. Show them that they are able to carry responsibility. Emphasise the need for teamwork, for give and take in the family. Encourage frank and open discussion about honesty and having a sense of responsibility. Role model how to apologise when you make a mistake, or don't get things right.

Remember, your job is to help them to learn and feel good about taking responsibility for their behaviour. When they achieve this, they will be able to take control of their future.

Emotional outbursts: the argument may not always be the real argument

In some ways, the young adults who shout and tell you exactly what they think of you are easier to deal with than those who withdraw and become passive aggressive. However if you shut down these outbursts with even tougher authority, there is a risk that your adolescent will suppress their words with the expectation that nobody will listen to them anyway, so what is the point? Feelings of resentment will go underground, sit there, and seethe unless the issue is addressed in a fair and calm manner at a later date. Not doing this can lead to passive aggressive behaviour.

What the adolescent wants is to grow up and become their own independent person. Argument is often about them convincing themselves that they are different to you. This helps them feel a degree of separation from you, and gives them a feeling of independence of mind. Attempts to express deep feelings will often come out in clumsy ways, even for adults. Have some understanding that this kind of expression is not easy for your teenager. Don't ridicule their outbursts; help them express what it is they feel deeply about and explain how they might have chosen to deal with the issue. If you repeatedly refuse to listen to what your adolescent wants to say, there is a danger that your adolescent will go underground with their feelings and refuse to speak his or her mind. This makes it really hard to make things better.

It is important that, as a parent, you take your defensive emotions out of the equation. No matter how hurt or how disappointed you feel, put this aside and realise that the issue is that your adolescent is struggling to cope with the tasks of growing up because they are going about it in ways that are not appropriate. Adolescents often equate defiance with independence. To help them along, show them that you are unaffected emotionally and ask them what they would really like to change. Make them take responsibility for what they are asking:

> 'I hear that you are frustrated, and think I am the worst person in the world, but until you can sit and talk to me calmly about some acceptable limits, I can't change that.'

> 'I hear that you want a new skateboard like all your mates, but I don't hear how you are prepared to contribute to our family. How about we work out a way you can get your skateboard by working for it?'

The ultimate emotional blackmail ... or a cry for help?

The ultimate blackmail of 'I'll just kill myself' is something no parent wants to hear. You might respond with something like, 'If you really feel like that and won't talk to us, we need to get you to a counsellor with whom you can talk through all your issues, and let us know how we can help you. If you are just annoyed because we won't let you stay late at the party, then let's sit down and talk in order to negotiate a reasonable plan that will gradually bring you that freedom'.

Again, it is important not to buy straight into the threat if your gut-feeling is that this is attention-seeking or emotional blackmail. If you believe your adolescent is seriously depressed then talk to them and ask if they feel comfortable talking through everything with you, or would rather talk to someone outside the family. If they are intent on seriously hurting themselves, call the mental health crisis line as soon as possible.

Depression is largely about unexpressed emotion. Adolescents often think that they are the only ones to have deep and complex feelings. They will state that they think adults, especially you as a parent, would not understand, and yet adolescents will be queued up at a counsellor's office to talk about all the things they feel deeply about. There have been many young people who have astounded me with their level of adult emotion and insight into the world in general. Young people love talking to someone older as long as the adult does not talk to them as if they were still a child.

The trouble here is that parents often relate to their adolescents in the same way they have been relating to them since they were small children. Adults can be forgiven for this because the shift to adult-like thinking and insight seems to happen very quickly. Within a few months your adolescent is no longer a child. It is like the brain hits a point of development where childlike thinking is suddenly diminished. It does not disappear altogether, but suddenly your 12- or 13-year-old will start to think with greater understanding of the world. It is hard for parents to clue into this sudden change.

If your adolescent is depressed, take time to talk to them. It might help to tell your adolescent about some of your struggles and show that you understand that life can sometimes be tough. Your adolescent needs to understand the nature of depression. They need to understand that depression will lift if they are courageous enough to speak out about what they are feeling.

Everyone experiences hurt. It is a part of living. When the feeling of hurt is pushed down with a rationalisation of, 'No big deal, I can handle this', it becomes 'held'. When subsequent hurt happens and the same process is applied over and over, the quantity of hurt feelings that have been suppressed become overwhelming, and people don't know why they are depressed. They have lost sight of all the hurts they have suppressed.

The need for assertion skills
The way out of depression is to start talking about all the things that have hurt in the past, regardless of how ridiculously small or big they happen to be. Depression will lift as you verbalise the things that upset you and work out strategies to do things

differently in the future. When adolescents are depressed, it is likely that their needs are not being met because they lack assertion skills.

If your adolescent is screaming and yelling to get what they want, it is likely that their hostility will only produce hostility in you. The hostility you feel prevents their needs being met. On the other hand, if your adolescent is being passive by refusing to say anything, this also prevents their needs being met. Your adolescent may need to learn to be assertive. This means being neither aggressive nor passive. It means learning to speak up and ask for what you want. It means learning to speak up straight away when something or someone hurts them. With assertive behaviour your adolescent will have a good chance of getting their needs met.

Encourage your teenager to use 'I' language. Suggest they start with saying exactly what they think about the situation. Suggest they acknowledge what they feel (at least to themselves) and then encourage them to say what they want, i.e. state what they prefer to happen in the future. Teach them in gradual steps to speak up about what they think, feel, and prefer to happen. Even better, role model this form of communication.

Crisis time

There are many dynamics a young person has to deal with in the school environment, and it is easy for them to feel overwhelmed. When they are struggling at school and are also in constant conflict at home, they will often report that they feel they can't do anything right, or that the world sucks. Low self-esteem, self-doubt, and feeling unloved makes young people vulnerable to seduction by individuals, peer groups, or sects. Kids drop out of school when they lack confidence in their ability.

On the home-front, parents report that the behaviour they are on the receiving end is untenable. As a counsellor talking to their teenager, I find there is always much more to the story. It is hard for young people to make the transition to adulthood, to suddenly become confident in expressing adult emotion. As they struggle for independence, they fear that relying once again on their parents to help them is a sign that they are still a child. Young people sometimes feel stuck, fearing that if they talk to their parents they will have to suffer their parents' overreaction like contacting their school principal or making a complaint when what they really want is strategies to deal with a particular situation on their own. Parents need to respect their adolescent's wishes unless, of course, there is physical danger involved or severe bullying.

Good schools will foster the notion that it is an adult thing to do to talk over issues in an adult way. They will encouage students to talk to a school counsellor if they don't feel they can talk to a teacher or their parent. In reality school counsellors work very hard to bridge any gap between parent and young person. Often it is as simple as getting the young person comfortable in talking with an adult, gaining confidence in their ability to express themselves and learning the kind of emotional language they need to be able to express themselves to their parents.

It is then a matter of coaching them in how to handle the conversation with their parents and how to deal with the likely reactions they might receive. Sometimes there are personal issues the young person wishes to keep to themselves. This is not a sign of a failing relationship with their parent. It is a sign that they are learning how to distinguish between what they need to communicate and what they wish to keep to themselves or share with a particular individual, just as adults do.

Encourage your adolescent to talk to a responsible adult. In your own words, assist them by telling them that you understand their need to sort things out on their own and explain that it is an adult thing to do to talk things over with someone. It might also be worth communicating that when they are ready to talk, you will be ready to help them in any way they need.

If the level of crisis is extreme, and your young person is staying out all night, into drugs, or graffiti, this is a much bigger issue that requires full examination of their life and social interactions. Sometimes it calls for total removal from their social situation in favour of seeing some of the world and having life experiences that change their outlook and build their self-esteem. Drastic situations can often require drastic solutions. Seek professional help yourself to manage this kind of crisis.

10

Step-parenting and blending families

10.1. Relationships in times of transition

10.2. Before you bring your new family unit together

10.3. Becoming a solid family unit

10.4. Step-parenting

10.5. Attitudes that impede positive adjustment

10.6. If disciplinary issues appear

10.7. When the family unit settles and life starts to feel good

10.1. Relationships in times of transition

Family groupings are diverse in gender, time, and geographical location. The presence of children in a relationship brings many added dimensions to relationship breakup. When a family breakup occurs, many families negotiate the fundamental changes in a calm and respectful way.

If you find yourself in a situation where you need to break up a relationship that brings no happiness for either partner, then take responsibility for that decision without blaming or disrespecting your soon to be ex-partner. It is not so much the crisis that has a lasting effect on children, but rather the manner in which you deal with it. The overwhelming need to exonerate yourself from blame in the eyes of your children will tempt behaviour that demeans or undermines your ex-partner. If you are in the situation of separating from your partner, know that it is not helpful to your children to blame or shame your ex. This needs to be discussed openly with your soon to be ex-partner.

It is natural to reflect on where things went wrong. Helpful reflections might include things like:

'Where did it start?'

'If only one partner had not done this then the other would not have done that'.

'Our beliefs and lifestyle choices are so different'.

'We have different interests, different tastes'.

'After our children grew we found we had nothing in common'.

'We have both made too many bad mistakes, there is no trust or respect anymore'.

If you separate, make sure you communicate sufficiently with your ex-partner until you reach a point of understanding. You both need to reach a place where there is an appreciation and understanding of all the fundamental differences that eventually made it difficult to sustain your relationship over the long-term. Presuming you both love your children, there must be an understanding of the need for both of you to remain friends and to co-parent respectfully. This requires each of you to respect the right of the other to be different. That is not to say that sadness goes away easily. It takes time. What is important is that the children benefit and likely thrive in the long term if both parents have the capacity to show respect for each other. This only happens when extensive communication takes place between the adults.

Children do not deserve to be pulled back and forth between you or to be put in the situation of trying to work out which adult is the 'bad' one. Children know when you are being honest or dishonest with them. They adapt well to a change in circumstance as long as they understand what is happening and why it has happened. When they know what to expect in their new setting, and both parents are saying the same thing to them, they can maintain a sense of security. Children of all ages appreciate honest and open dialogue.

10.2. Before you bring your new family unit together

The kind of journey experienced in new family groupings is often determined at the outset by the manner in which the previous relationship breakup has been managed. Whether it is a mutual breakup, or a situation where one partner forces the separation, it is the way in which each partner behaves towards the other in front of the children that sets the scene for the future. When a breakup occurs there is a natural grief cycle with all the elements of loss that occur when someone dies. The family unit as it has been experienced comes to an end. When ex-partners continue to blame each other, this grief period lasts longer.

When communication has broken down and one of the partners has resorted to violence, verbal abuse, or demeaning behaviour, the children are often subjected to a nightmare existence. Their world is turned upside-down, and if this is not bad enough, the parents can become so obsessed with getting back at their ex-partner that their children lose out on love and affection when they need it most.

Breakups don't need to be brutal. If your relationship breaks down, the prime concern needs to be for the welfare of the children. Every person in the family has to accept and adjust to a new life situation. There are many emotions that need to be communicated and worked through. Children need to be helped to understand the adjustments they will need to make, and their emotions must be held lovingly as they move through them. Children and teenagers need the security of two parents who they know confidently will love and care for them, no matter what the unknown future brings. Sometimes this requires adults to be selfless. Before you bring your new family unit together, take time out to discuss some of the following with your new partner.

Physical space
With a new partner and new family grouping, a sense of confusion can set in, with the adults finding that this is not the ideal family life they had initially dreamed. There are often more children and less space. Teenagers may express feeling invaded and fussed by younger children, with nowhere to escape to. They find they are having less conversation with their parent than in their previous biological family. When there are new members in the family it takes a while for the social dynamics to settle. Being with new people all the time can be a strain. Kids may not even have the words to express how they feel about this new situation, and they can come out with some strange complaints that seem quite irrelevant. As in most situations, talking helps. Special time with the biological parent helps, as do places for personal withdrawal from the business of the new family unit.

Emotional space
Kids need emotional space. Constant talking and sharing of feelings can be overwhelming. I have seen new partners determined to create a relationship with their partner's children that is the same as with their own children. Teenagers hate being forced to talk about their feelings and they resent the intrusion on their emotional space. It may take a long time for kids to feel comfortable talking about their feelings with a step-parent. They may not welcome hugs from a step-parent. These things have to happen naturally.

When resentment builds up, emotional manipulation can result. Situations can be misrepresented to the other parent about a step-parent, or vice versa. Untrue or biased stories

10. Step-parenting and blending families

can be reported back to the other biological parent. This is a great way for a child either to put a wedge between the newly partnered adults or to gain some kind of leverage with the other parent. In this case, all the adults involved need to be open and trusting of each other, without buying into manipulations.

Communication and information privacy
When there are children at various ages and stages there can be great opportunities for family communication, like at meal times. These occasions give opportunity to develop a sense of belonging, affirmation, and communal fun. At other times, kids and adults need to have an option to withdraw into their own space. Parents also need to be free to talk with each other privately.

When there are members of the family who dominate, others can feel they never get a word in. Other members of the family may habitually say nothing. If the stepdad is there and always silent, how do the kids get to know him? It is worth analysing how communication happens in the family and how decisions will be made. Who consults who? Does one parent take responsibility for the final decisions about their own biological child, or are those decisions shared? Which decisions are made only by adults, which are made by the whole family, and which are made by the kids who make the loudest noise?

There needs to be respect for privacy around personal information for both adults and children. A child may not want you to tell the rest of the family their blood test results, or school results, or the fact that they got a special text from their first boyfriend. Confidentiality needs to be articulated and respected. At the same time, with busy families it is easy for some members to miss out on vital information, routines, and plans. Simple strategies like a message board need to be developed to overcome this.

At the end of the day, what is important for children or teenagers is that they have two parents they can respect, parents who they see as good role models. If parents lack this insight, the child is drawn away from the experience of having two parents who love them. It is tough! When parents choose to abandon their children because they can't cope with the stress and backstabbing caused by the ex-partner, it is the children who miss out and there is often a legacy of long-term mental health issues for the child who interprets their parent's absence as personal rejection. The sense of rejection can persist as a life theme. Children need access to both parents.

Even when one parent lives at a distance, children will often smile broadly and say, 'Dad always remembers to send me a birthday present'. Regular and reliable contact is important. The simple acknowledgment of love is enough to help them hang onto the belief that they are loved by both parents. For some children whose only hope of connection is that their estranged parent will send them a birthday present, it is so sad to see the way they feel rejected yet again.

10.3. Becoming a solid family unit

In the beginning there is often a fantasy stage where new partners have glowing ideas about what a wonderful blended family they will create together while at the same stage the kids are still fantasising about their own Mum and Dad getting back together. The journey of blended families can sometimes be smooth, and sometimes difficult. In the adjustment phase, it is important that adults talk with kids about how they are finding the new living arrangements, and be prepared to dig a little deeper without being defensive or reactive to what the kids are saying. What is important is that they are expressing themselves rather than the content of what they are saying. Try not to take the criticism personally.

While new routines develop quickly, it generally takes a couple of years for all members of a stepfamily to accept the new situation as permanent and stable. The acceptance of the new partner does not depend simply on whether the person is 'liked', or seen as a good person. The incoming partner needs the ability to be sensitive to the needs of the parent-child relationship, and to take a back seat when needed. For the biological parent in this new family arrangement, much skill is required to juggle responsibilities and relationships, especially when children are only partially resident. It is a tough call all round. There is often a strong temptation to undermine the other separated partner. Adults will often think that subtlety goes over a child's head. Not so. Children are particularly astute to such nuances. Adults aware of this will also use nuance to influence their children because it gives them a superficial defence, that they never said anything outright that was negative about their ex-partner or that the child got it wrong. They kid themselves.

It is a hard enough challenge in a child-free marriage to work through the numerous differences in culture and lifestyle that each partner brings to the relationship. It is often hard in a stable, conjugal family to negotiate parenting techniques and behaviour expectations. When a new partner steps into a pre-existing culture they likely experience something akin to walking through a minefield, with unexpected explosions underfoot. When the explosions occur, and conflict rises, make sure you allow time for tempers to calm. Seek each party's willingness to resolve the issue. Hear each side of the argument, and strive collaboratively for a win-win situation. Accept that conflict is normal in any team situation. Have confidence in your ability to work through the conflict in a way that each person feels heard, validated, and accepting of the outcome.

The closer the new family's routine is to the old one, the easier life will be. While this can seem frustrating for a new step-parent, it is important to go with the flow and gradually modify down the track. Be considerate of the children. With well-established routines, duplication of important items, and respectful consideration, young people often report that life is smooth and easy. They enjoy the stimulation of moving from one situation to another. They have more adults to relate to. They receive attention from four adults instead of two, and often have stepsisters or stepbrothers to play with. Life can be fun and full of stimulation as each family experiences various adventures and events, however, there are often practical concerns that make their lives complex.

Biological parents will argue that they each want time with their child during the week, as well as weekends. In some contexts they fail to consider the inconvenience for the child. When there is lots of unexpected movement between Mum's and Dad's home, the lack of routine demands the kids be exceedingly well-organised and responsible. One may argue that this is a good thing, however, by high school kids find all this tiring and frustrating, always having to think ahead. They like to have their own patch, their own computer to talk to friends, and their own emotional space.

When life is chaotic, children and adolescents often report that they hate having to go from one family to another. It is too much trouble! Lunch boxes, homework, craft pieces, projects, precious stationery, books, birthday presents, and clothes all need to be remembered and carted to and from school. These kinds of practicalities need to be discussed and thrashed out with your adolescent so that life's requirements remain as simple and routine as possible. If it means the teenager spends extra nights with Mum or Dad, and understands that the choice is for their own convenience, they will be fully accepting and appreciate the consideration given to them.

10.4. Step-parenting

The term 'step-parent' is an out-of-date term that used to refer to the person who took the place of a deceased parent. 'Stepmother' brings with it negative connotations to begin with, conjuring images of wicked and evil, yet, there are many stepmothers and stepfathers who take on enormous responsibilities and provide lovingly for children who are not biologically their own. It is unfortunate that we do not seem to have a more positive English word to describe the very complex and positive roles that stepfathers and stepmothers play in the life of children from separated parents.

10. Step-parenting and blending families

For many, the transition to stepfamily life is often smooth and easy, with both biological parents working for the benefit of the children. They put aside their hurt and disharmony because they are both determined that their children will not suffer because of their own marital breakdown. They agree on arrangements, creating routines that engender security in the children. When this happens, after the initial adjustment period, children report that life is good. They have plenty of time with both Mum and Dad. They seem to deal better with the grief of having lost the family unit as they knew it. Children adapt well to new routines because their sense of time is different to adults. Chaotic arrangements or lack of routine is what brings insecurity.

Some children and teenagers find it difficult to adjust to a new family group situation, a situation that has not been of their making. There can be many aspects of the adjustment that cause distress. For the adult or the child there can be changes in lifestyle that inevitably result in some kind of inconvenience. Needs are not met as easily as they were previously. Children can feel a sense of rejection and have difficulty finding their place in the new family unit. It is hard for them to understand the complexity of emotion, and the transition period can be quite rocky if there is not adequate communication about the myriad of feelings experienced in the background.

Sometimes it is not enough to love and reassure a child. Children need to understand what they can ask for and what they can expect. Each child has a different personality and will react in a different way. Some will be open-hearted and loving toward the new step-parent. Others will be cautious, or even resentful. The child's personality also affects the quality of the new family relationships. Adults have to find ways to listen to their child's concerns and allow them to shape their perspective and attitude towards the new family configuration. There is no one way to assure children that they are loved. They need to experience the love for themselves.

Dependent on the personality mix, it is quite possible that your step-children will take a natural liking to you. You may find that they share your interests, enjoy your company, and become forever close to you. If this is not the case, your role as a step-parent is about being willing to love, support, and assist. Beyond that, any stance of emotional investment or expectation might be fraught with disappointment and resentment. If you maintain your own integrity, this will shine through in the end and your stepchild will eventually see you as an honourable person thrust into a difficult role. It always takes two to create relationship and your step-children play an equal part in that.

In the initial stages, when a step-parent comes into a family with existing teenage children, courage is needed to accept the little emotional 'slaps in the face' as adolescents or children lash out at an easy target. Adjustment takes time and little hurts can be expected. Part of this is about kids wanting to see how you react. If you react badly, that is fuel for their discontent. If you react in a kind and caring way, this is confusing to them. They may simply accept you as you are or they may test limits with discipline. Step-parents often report that they feel they can never compete with the bond that already exists between parent and child, and yet there should never be a competition. Being a step-parent is a unique relationship that simply cannot be compared to the bond that exists between a parent and their child. A life partnership with your new partner is also something that stands on its own and prevails long past the years spend in parenting. The two should never be compared. Children eventually lead their own lives. Their ability to grow up and become independent has its basis in secure relationship with their parents.

The bond between a parent and child has to be preserved at all cost. I have seen children struggle because the new partner seems to be number one in Mum or Dad's eyes. It is foolish to engage in this kind of competition. It is never easy, at any age, to step back and give priority to the child's needs. Step-parenting is a role that requires fortitude and an acceptance of the requirement to give, without any expectation of return. It is a role that requires stability and maturity. On those occasions where you find you are able to make a worthwhile contribution, let the sense of your own integrity be sufficient reward.

10.5. Attitudes that impede positive adjustment

Children often worry about the parent they leave behind. If this parent is upset, irritated, or negative about the child going into the other parent's care, it has a huge impact on the child. The child begins to feel guilty if they do enjoy themselves, and can set about making sure it is not an enjoyable time. This whole situation is exacerbated if either parent contributes to the child's sense of guilt by declaring their loneliness, or how much they miss the child.

When new stepfamilies form, each member brings with them some preconception about how life will be. This can be an expectation of loss and dread, or it can be a rose-coloured fantasy akin to *The Brady Bunch*. As the family gets to know each other, likes and dislikes grow in number, coalitions are formed that can be positive, and others can serve to divide and rule. Adults need to be on the lookout for emotional manipulations that children can design to set a parent or step-parent against each other.

When the separated parent living apart from the new stepfamily expresses excessive disdain for the new partnership, kids can feel blinded to any positive aspects of their new situation. There can be a tendency to measure time, love, kindness, and hurt with incredible precision. They keep score. Love might be measured by the size of a present. It is so sad when this happens. Ultimately, with time children come to see through the negative lens given to them by their parent who has not accepted the change graciously. They come to see the new family members realistically.

If you are dealing with a difficult ex-partner you need to trust your children will eventually change their attitude. You need to avoid lowering your behaviour and your attitude to mirror that of your ex-partner. You need to remain confident that your offspring will observe your integrity and will turn their own attitudes around, valuing you for your decent behaviour. Be solid in yourself, and extremely patient. It might take months or years before your children start to see things how they really are. Know that at the end of the day you have done all you can.

Children and teenagers feeling pushed aside

Children and adolescents can be adamant that their mother cares more about her new partner than she does about them. While this is probably not true, their experience often tells them that Mum has rarely had time for them since the new partner moved in. Similarly, their experience tells them that Dad is more interested in his new partner's kids. The loyalty battle is a big one, and it is quite common for each member of a stepfamily to express extreme frustration and deep feelings of not belonging, while the adults simply tread water trying to meet all demands and keep the new family unit afloat. Young children from the new partnership grow into the world, looking up to and idolising their older sisters and brothers. They have no understanding of family dynamics or the resentments held. It can be confusing to them as one minute they are the centre of attention, only to be pushed away as resentments emerge in their older sister or brother.

Sometimes these resentments are fuelled by a parent and stepparent who insist that the new stepfamily does everything together. Great in theory, but in practice the child feels like they can never have their parent alone. Children need time alone with each of their parents, and parents need to assure their kids that they will make special time to spend with each one of them. Managing all this can be a complex scheduling task. There are many competing demands in a blended family. The logistics can seem overwhelming. What is important is that special time is on the agenda and has importance equal to other aspects of daily life.

Beneath all the self-centredness, adolescents frequently express a real frustration that they no longer have any time alone with their parent. While some take this to the extreme of being highly demanding, others report that they feel genuinely cast aside as the parent gets all carried away with the new love of their life. Small bursts of time alone with a parent easily solves this disgruntled feeling, however, when the parent involved is insecure or controlling, this feeling does not get addressed. It is the quality of the connection that happens in this time that is critical, not the quantity of time spent.

Adolescents taking things into their own hands

Life in a stepfamily can be fun and exhilarating. Alternatively, it can become fraught with jealousy, torn loyalties, hurt, and confusion. Adolescents will frequently report that everything was okay until 'he' or 'she' moved in, especially when the parent and adolescent have been together and on their own for a long time. The adolescent resents the newcomer to the family, and will sometimes go to incredible lengths to let that person know they are not welcome. It is hard to listen when adolescents tell me all the nasty little tricks they have played on their step-parent. They will often chuckle and roll their eyes when the step-parent takes a stance, objecting to the adolescent's behaviour. Through the adolescent's eyes, the step-parent takes on the face of a monster, ever looming over and destroying the adolescent's otherwise happy life. Of course, adolescents see things from their own perspective where less of Mum's immediate attention equates to the 'monster stepfather', or less of Dad's attention equates to 'monster stepmother'.

Adolescents can be very astute in their observation of immaturity and selfishness in parents. They can present wonderful insights like, 'Mum was lonely and jumped into the new relationship because he took her places, when Dad never did. But he is mean and she can't see it!' Sometimes adolescents will state openly that they don't want their parent to have anyone special if it is not their natural mother and father. They always look very surprised when I comment, 'Oh, so you are quite happy to keep your mum company for the next 10 years on a Saturday night, or to stay home and stroke her hand as you watch old-fashioned movies with her?'

'No!' they gasp.

I say, 'Then maybe it is a good thing that Mum or Dad have someone to keep them happy, and look after them when they are sick because you will be wanting to live your own life in just a few years'.

Of course, as parents and step-parents stretch themselves between their new love, their children, their job, household duties, and personal recreation, it is easy for a moment's connection to be swallowed up in organisational and transactional issues. The biggest mistake new blended families make is to expect that all should and will get along instantly. It takes time, thought, reflection, mindful scheduling, considerable communication, and determination to push through the difficulties and value the positive aspects of the new situation. Adolescents may push the boundaries and want to move out. They need to feel loved and wanted and they need to communicate their difficulties without the biological parent losing patience. While tempering their self-centredness, adolescents have to gain something from being a part of their new family constellation. With patience and kindness, everyone in the family will eventually come around to acceptance of their new situation.

What adolescents fail to realise is that the step-parent is really the 'outsider'. While the adolescent feels excluded from this new close relationship, it does not occur to them that the bond they have with their parent is biologically far stronger than any bond their parent may have with a partner. Partners can come and go over a lifetime, whereas once a child, always a child. You are always connected to your parent unless you choose otherwise. It is not something that is easily destroyed. Step-parents must be very conscious of this bond. Adolescents also need to appreciate how it must feel for their step-parent to feel like an interloper. Adolescents need to be calmly brought into a reality where they realise that it is not just about them. Each member of the blended family needs to be emotionally cared for and looked after.

The biological parent outside the new family unit
How tough it is to have had full-time care of your children, only to pass them over to part-time residence with the other biological partner and new step-parent. This is not a scenario that adults envisage when they set out on the path of having children. Sudden changes throw everyone into shock, and adults need to be sensitive to the need for gradual introduction of new parenting arrangements. It is beneficial for everyone if

10. Step-parenting and blending families

there is a gradual time increase rather than sudden demands for half-time access. Consider the welfare of the ex-partner. If your ex-partner is devastated by sudden change, this will not play out well for your children. Once again, let the welfare of your children be your guide to a natural and a gradual transition into the new stepfamily. Accept that a transition is happening, that things will never go back to the way they were. Seek professional support to help you through this testing and difficult transition.

If you find yourself in the position of being the aggrieved parent, consider the impact of your behaviour on your children. Think about what you want for them and choose how you want to be. Bitterness, jealousy, and undermining behaviour only serve to destroy the ability of children to relax, enjoy, and adapt to their new living arrangements. It is easier said than done. It is the toughest test of parenting to be able to manage this transition in a mature way, putting the needs of the children ahead of your own. Feeding children with negative attitudes towards their other family situation destroys their chance of happiness. Your children will not be happy if they know you are unhappy.

When the stepfamily situation is not going so well, children often have nowhere to go for support. If they return home unhappy from their step family stay they are likely to upset the home parent or refuel the negativity that this parent holds towards the other step family. On the other hand, if the kids return home feeling really happy and exuberant, they might also upset the home parent. Kids often find themselves in a no-win situation. It is so important that some adult issues are not shared with children.

I have seen the greatest and most lingering anguish when one parent assumes victim status in the eyes of their children. They truly believe that the parent who left the house is the villain. These children are, in effect, brainwashed by the victim-like parent and often carry negative beliefs into adult life. I have seen mothers and fathers become suicidal because they have been so maligned by their ex-partner that their children have disowned them. The aggrieved parent finds themselves in a no-win situation. If they stand up for themselves and malign the other parent to the children, then they are dragging the children into nasty bitterness. If they say nothing, they are distanced because there is no way to defend themselves. Either way, they are in a no-win situation. When one parent finds the other biological parent too difficult to deal with, they sometimes give up trying to have reasonable negotiation because the stress has such a negative impact on their health and emotional wellbeing. They either feel excluded or exclude themselves sometimes for the benefit of themselves and sometimes for the benefit of their children.

This is really tough. When children grow and finally meet their excluded parent, there are a number of complex issues that arise. Often the child reports feeling that the excluded parent did not try hard enough or that they felt abandoned. Sometimes they will say 'They are both as bad as each other. I am over them'.

Children grow to be wise adults who come to see exactly what each parent is truly like, but it is a long time to wait and an arduous journey. If you find yourself in this situation, know that you will need considerable fortitude to get through. Eventually your moment will come. It will be a lightbulb moment for your children when they realise that you are not the kind of person painted by their other biological parent. When they realise what has been happening, they can turn away from the biological parent who misrepresented the situation to them. Think carefully about how you conduct yourself in regard to the other parent of your children. Think about the outcomes you want and choose how you want to be.

The frustrations of the estranged parent
Estranged and excluded parents often report total frustration with the fact that while they already pay support to the custodial parent, they have no control or influence over the level of spending that takes place. Estranged parents may live at a distance, be paying child maintenance, and yet have minimal or no access to their children.

10. Step-parenting and blending families

Parents often feel estranged when they are treated poorly by an ex-partner who is very controlling with access. These parents will report that they often have to purchase clothes, pay for extra-curricular activities, entertain in holidays, and pay for haircuts and dental visits because the custodial parent does not provide these. One client reported that the child always arrived without their epilepsy medication. This was intentional, just to make the necessary visit to the GP an inconvenience. Children are sometimes manipulated, being told that 'Dad never pays enough for your care'. For the new partner, there can be resentment of constant outgoing of money that seems to be taken for granted. The results of jealousy, adult greediness, and a need to control or influence what transpires can be a huge source of tension for new partners who are desperately trying to make their new family arrangement work.

Adults can also find that they are on an emotional rollercoaster ride with each visit. They typically report that life just begins to feel really good by Sunday night when it is time for the kids to go home again. For the step parent, it can be a long-term juggling act to cope with the special emotional bonds that exist outside the partnership and the exclusion they feel from step children. Rejection is a powerful tool to get the step-parent offside. It can come with simple statements like, 'I don't want [X] to come', subtle ignoring, or 'I don't care if it is his birthday.

With strong parent-child emotional bonds come demands that always impact on the new adult relationship. They are so intrinsic to the parent-child relationship that they can become a blind spot, a chasm in which the biological parent cannot understand their new partner's perspective, thinking that their partner is being a little precious, or over the top. What they fail to understand is that it is tough being in a step-parent role and to feel excluded from this precious parent-child relationship. This difficulty needs to be acknowledged and supported.

A typical scenario is where the biological parent in the new family unit spoils or favours a particular child but is unaware that he/she does it. When the step-parent sees this clearly and conflict evolves, the parent may feel he/she has to choose between the child and the partner. This can become a gut-wrenching situation. Spoilt children do not fare well, so much discussion needs to take place about what is best for the children. If there is favouritism, there has to be honest and open discussion about the reasons for this. There has to be trust that both partners want what is best for the children. It takes a very strong partnership to handle the tug of war that can emerge within the new family setting, even when the ex-partner is reasonable and co-operative.

One couple I saw reported that they were in total anguish over whether they should fight for more custody/access of the husband's daughter. The daughter lived with her mother who treated the custody battle as a power struggle to serve her own needs, rather than the needs of the daughter. She would fill the girl's head with all kinds of negativity towards the father. She had demonstrated such nasty game-playing that the couple truly could not decide whether a court battle would exacerbate the problem or whether they were being neglectful if they did not fight for custody of the child. It seemed to be a no-win situation. While most adults handle family break-ups well, this story is, unfortunately, not uncommon.

In the final analysis, most of the destructive influences on blended families evolve from a fundamental belief that when a relationship does not last there must be blame attached. When parents move to a healthy acceptance of their relationship breakup, issues for the children are minimised.

10.6. If disciplinary issues appear

Just as families begin to navigate through the myriad of issues and start to find their feet with routines, adjusted expectations, and verbal expression of wants and needs, discipline issues sometimes begin to appear. This is almost a sign of normal family life, however, it is often experienced as a sense of chaos, as if life is falling apart. Previously compliant young ones start acting out, and adults start to experience fatigue.

New step-parents often report extreme frustration at not being able to discipline children and adolescents, especially when the biological parent fails to discipline from fear that the child will reject or distance them. If the step-parent does discipline, he/she can be seen as intruding on the parent-child relationship. Some children will act out and become violently abusive towards the step-parent, while others will withdraw but play passive-agressive exclusion games, such as ignoring the presence of the step-parent, or going out of the way to omit and exclude the step-parent in any act of giving. Much of what happens depends on the solidarity of the relationship between the parent and the step-parent. Where there is fragility, children will often exploit it in order to gain what they are being refused. When the parent and step-parent stand together on well-explained consequences, there is nothing to exploit and consequences have to be accepted.

When children or adolescents feel resentment towards either parent, it is a raw pain that opens up periodically and gets mixed up in discipline issues. From the painful position of childhood, there is very often a limited understanding of why Mummy or Daddy left. Children will blame themselves, thinking that if they had been less naughty then their parents may not have fought or separated. From the painful position of adolescents, life is hard enough as it is without the adults making everything more difficult. It is often not until adult life that individuals look back and identify their own perspectives as a little egocentric.

Discipline is often a 'no-no' for step-parents, as they often feel they have to be accepted and acknowledged first before taking on a disciplinary role. It is also very tricky stepping into a disciplinary relationship that is pre-existing. Asserting oneself in this situation is tantamount to insurgence on the one hand, or the 'wicked step-parent' on the other. There is another aspect of this for the step-parent. Unless they are present from the time the children are babies, step-parents often express that there is nothing they can do to feel fully accepted, that they feel second-class and unappreciated no matter how involved they become. They often express that they feel used, financially and emotionally, yet, I have also had many young clients who weep over the loss of their step-parent for whom they express great love and respect. Family discussion needs to occur around specific rules and the need for either parent or step-parent to step in if the rules are broken. When unusual, new or particularly contentious issues present themselves, then the step-parent and parent may agree that these should be deferred to the parent.

It is always difficult when parents have different beliefs about discipline, regardless of the family situation. It is quite common for one parent to perceive his or her relationship with the child to be so fragile that he or she dare not discipline. The failure to discipline gives rise to demanding behaviour, and inevitably becomes a source of conflict with the new partner. It exacerbates the tension level within both families. The parent's fear underlying this behaviour is very real: 'What if my child doesn't want to see me again? I can't risk that!' The trouble is, this often leads to the child being overindulged. In reality, in the worst case scenario, if the child does reject the parent because they can't get their own way, it really needs to be regarded as a major tantrum that will eventually ease, as tantrums do.

What parents in this situation fail to realise is that children will love their parent as long as that relationship is free from demeaning or abusive behaviour. A good relationship is not lost because the child tantrums. Good, firm discipline assists children by creating boundaries within which they feel secure. A relationship without these is stressful and confusing for children, and it makes their world limitless and scary. Discipline that has appropriate consequences, rather than punishment, re-affirms the boundaries that reflect the larger boundaries in the 'big world'. It is very sad when there is so little cooperation between estranged parents that children miss this positive source of discipline. The world is a harder place for them to navigate.

Different beliefs, standards, and expectations open the door for children to become manipulative and able to fuel the other parent's angst. It is important for parents to verbalise a respect for the differences that occur in other families. Children quickly learn how to behave in different circumstances. They are extremely adaptable. Where there is disrespect between estranged parents, children see this as an opportunity to act out, to become emotionally manipulative, and to behave in ways that please one parent and anger the other. They learn to distort the truth for personal gain. Life is very different when biological parents and even step-parents can communicate respectfully with each other and work together for the welfare of their children.

10.7. When the family unit settles and life starts to feel good

Each blended family develops its own unique culture, but this takes time. Eventually there is a sense of stability where everyone knows what to expect in their family life. Even when the road is rocky, there are opportunities for growth if they are recognised.

It is the way that conflict is dealt with that either frees or imprisons within the culture. Fear of expressing hurt drives resentment underground, away from authentic connection, the very thing that will bind the new family. Children often need to be helped to identify what it is they are feeling. The situation is new, the feelings are new, and kids don't necessarily have the words they need. It is the space to allow the expression of hurt, and the expression of gratitude that opens the door to new relationships. Too often the step-parent will draw away rather than open themselves up to the hurt they feel. Too often the biological parent will be fearful of laying down well-conceived new rules and expectations for fear of inflaming the hostility.

Children thrive on limits. They find security in knowing what is what. They feel comforted by rules that command respect and consideration for others. At this stage, step-parents don't have to accept little slaps in the face. Their place in the family is cemented and their need for respect is equal to the other members of the family. Good relationships rarely happen instantly. They need time to create a good history of relating. Good moments of truth and caring alongside fun experiences together create bonds within the new family grouping.

It is wonderful when an adolescent says, 'I really like my step-parent. We get along really well'. And there are many relationships where both sets of parents get along well for the purposes of parenting the children. In other cases, where parental relationships are characterised by conflict, jealousy, and game-playing, there is a negativity that grows like poison. It saddens me greatly when I have to say to an adolescent that it is really not fair that their parent is using them to get at the ex-partner, and I have to teach strategies that require them to behave more maturely than their parents. A young person has to be assertive, honest, and confident to be able to request their father stop saying negative things about their mother, or vice versa.

Even where relationships are reasonably harmonious within stepfamilies, children and adolescents in particular will often verbalise their grief. They wish for a normal, ideal family with Mum and Dad at home together. They often make it a really tough time for themselves, resenting their situation rather than counting their blessings. When grief is evident, you need to be patient and understand that it will run its course. In time, these well-loved children inevitably meet up with someone who has had a far tougher life, prompting an insight that their stepfamily is not so bad.

Stepfamilies will often report that it has taken a couple of years to move away from their unrealistic fantasies about how wonderful life would be, through a period of feeling unsettled, confused, and shamed by the explosions of hurt, to a position of acceptance and celebration of everything working well. Each member of a stepfamily emerges with their own unique perspective on how their needs are either met or denied. There

10. Step-parenting and blending families

is an acceptance of different perspectives, but a bond of love and caring that makes them seem less significant. The point is that members of the family are able to speak their minds openly. They start to accept responsibility for at least hearing another perspective, even if they do not agree with it. Sadly, some stepfamilies never reach this stage.

In those situations where malice has been put aside for the sake of the children, and where parents treat each other with respect, it seems that children can thrive on the stimulation that comes from living in two households. Children cope quite well if they see their parents together as friendly human beings, if not together in a relationship.

As children and adolescents grow, they develop a very clear understanding of all the adults in their life. They can identify their good points, as well as their bad ones. The reality of the complexity of adult life brings with it some understanding of the potential fragility of any relationship, and often brings remarks like, 'I can't understand how they ever got together in the first place'. As adults they make their own judgements based on what they know of their parents in adult life.

This thought needs to be held onto steadfastly as each adult strives to do the best they can for the children. Eventually, there comes a sense of commitment where alliances are formed and important relationships appreciated. Many a time have I counselled young people who have been totally devastated at the loss of a step-parent who they say was more of a parent to them than their biological one. Given time, relationships come to stand on their own merit.

11

Grief, transition and change

11.1. Life inevitably brings grief

11.2. Emotional reactions and protracted grief

11.3. On taking grief home

11.4. Life is about persistence and living with uncertainty

11.1. Life inevitably brings grief

There can be grief in every aspect of life. The loss of a loved one is the first we think of, but grief often comes with letting go of the past while we adapt to the new changes in our lives. It can come with the letting go of old habits and behaviours, even the destructive ones. It can come with the letting go of old attitudes and old dreams.

A state of transition will also bring grief. It may be from the old job to the new job, from a state of loneliness to a relationship, from adolescence to adulthood. When you move into a state of transition or change, it seems to happen at a relatively acceptable pace, because you know what is happening. When there is a sudden loss, however, you are thrust into a state of shock and denial. It may be loss of job, loss of history as we knew it, loss of a loved one, or loss of a relationship. Sudden loss throws you unexpectedly into grief.

While it is easy to be glib and say that grief is just a part of life, the reality of grief can be profound. Sometimes it takes months or years for people to regain a sense of wellbeing. The first anniversary of a death seems to be a marking point that clients struggle through to gradually begin to feel better. It is not comfortable to feel a gap in your life, a gap left by someone or something. It takes a lot of courage to reassess one's life, to accept what 'is' rather than constantly reel about what 'is not'. It takes determination and persistence to rebuild a new life.

The experience of losing someone close is devastating. It is comforting that we never have to lose the sense of a loved one's spirit. The essence of your loved one can stay with you forever. Memories can bring comfort and joy in times when you are missing your loved one. Some report experiencing a spiritual connection with those who have passed. There are many explanations and revelations about death and near-death experiences. Creations of the mind? Creations from the need to believe? Maybe. I know that the unknown attracts projections of all kinds, and yet I remember driving over the Tasman Bridge and being overcome by an incredibly powerful feeling. It was something I still cannot describe; I had never had anything like it before, or since. When I arrived home my husband had just received a phone call informing us of my father's death.

While visiting Lady Elliott Island, a very long way from his home in Hobart, our five-year old grandson decided to build a coral garden for his special friend, Russel, our much loved elderly neighbour who had died a few months earlier. Later, we were told the location of our grandson's coral garden was one of Russell's favourite haunts as a young man, where he used to love mooring his boat. Experiences like this are very hard to explain away as simple coincidence.

The attributes we cherish in our loved ones can and do live on in those left behind. Only by dealing with it, rather than denying the emptiness of grief, can we move to a place of acceptance where the loved one is permanently in our soul and becomes part of what makes up our daily living. Sometimes it is hard to

11. Grief, transition and change

move to this place of acceptance on your own. Family help, or help from a professional counsellor will assist you to talk about your loss and gradually move through your own personal set of emotions to a place of acceptance. This is a place where you can celebrate the reality of your loved one's life, the good and the bad, and all that the person was. If you are finding it too hard to grieve then you need to take responsibility for yourself by reaching out for assistance. If you prolong the dampening of your spirit by denying the emotion of grief it can affect your health and your relationships. It is critical that you move through grief into an emotional place where you can once again enjoy your own journey.

If you are grieving you will probably experience familiar patterns associated with the process of grief. Shock, denial, anger, emotional ups and downs that gradually give way to acceptance of the loss, and reconciliation of what may have been against the reality of what is. Guilt over what has or has not been said is inevitable, since death is rarely timely. It is a process of coming to terms with a change that has already occurred.

Grief is deeply personal, and is a reminder of your own mortality. Grief is exhausting. The loss of a parent, in particular, reminds you that you are now approaching the latter part of your own life. Grief always teaches you to reassess your priorities in life. We all have a limited time on Earth, and the loss of a loved one is also a stark reminder to value and engage in the living yet to be done. Rather than engulf yourself in loneliness, you can choose to connect with and cherish those still physically with you.

Grief can be cumulative. If it is not dealt with at the time of loss, it can sit and remain in your emotional reservoir. One can never be sure what trigger will unleash that reservoir, and hence there are many who shy away or lock themselves out of situations involving grief emotion. The only way to deal with grief is to experience it, to allow it to happen naturally, to allow yourself to cry. If you let your emotion out, you will move through it. You will move from feelings of shock and denial to the highs and lows of emotion, where you might swing quickly from humorous memories to feelings of desolation. There are many ranges of emotion that take place. They are all normal reactions that can eventually give way to feelings of acceptance and peace.

For children, grief can be quite a frightening experience. Adolescents who experience grief for the first time can go into a panic response, truly believing that they will remain in grief for the rest of their lives. When adolescents observe adults who find it very difficult to talk about grief, it reinforces their fear.

I recall a time working in a high school when I was trying to get staff to take on Mind Matters, a national mental health program. After a period of time teachers reported they had taken on various units, though none had taken on the Grief unit. Why not? Is grief such a private emotion that we cannot speak of it? My guess was that teachers were anxious they might access their own past grief and be unable to remain emotionally in control. We invited a mental health officer to speak about grief to staff, and following that session, one teacher developed a wonderful English unit for Year 9 students on dealing with the death of a pet. She had identified a great opportunity to teach kids about grief.

Parents will often try to protect their children from every kind of grief experience instead of educating them and preparing them for serious grief that will inevitably happen at some stage in their life. If children can learn at an early age about the pattern of emotions that come with grief, then grief becomes familiar territory that they know they will move through. Their first experience of being in major grief will not be so terrifying.

Notions that hamper the movement through grief
There are some common notions that hamper the movement through grief. Kids report being fearful of forgetting the loved one's face. Some will be in a rush to remember everything, staying up all night in fear of forgetting things. This can be relentless and exhausting. If you are having difficulty

redirecting your brain to more peaceful places, try writing a journal or recording some of the things you don't want to forget. Sort pictures or document things that will relieve your brain from having to remember everything.

After a period of intense grief, some people feel guilty if they have a temporary lapse in their grieving where they forget all about the loved one. They have a feeling of having been disloyal. Daily life calls for functionality; it is not sustainable to feel guilt for not thinking of your loved one every minute of the day. You must give yourself permission to keep living, even though you still need to grieve. When you are ready, continue with your daily work and if you need time out to have a good cry, then do so.

If you are feeling consumed by your grief and can't concentrate on your daily work, it might help to allocate a certain time of the day when you know you will be free to grieve. You might like to go to a special place. You might like to use that time to write in your journal or metaphorically talk to the loved one you have lost. Some people like to have their own personal farewell ceremony where they find a special place to say the things they were never able to say, to say goodbye. Some like to complete a project in memory of their loved one.

11.2. Emotional reactions and protracted grief

Families who experience loss often find it hard to understand why the members of their family all seem to be behaving in different ways. It is a difficult time that requires restraint and respect. Everyone grieves at different rates and in different ways, and it is important that family members show respect and tolerance to each other.

What is important is that everyone moves through grief, rather than deny it. Some will say that you never cease to grieve, but the number of tears you shed and the frequency of those tears reduce over time and tough memories give way to recalling happy times with the loved one. When someone pushes grief aside and refuses to feel sad there can be a change in behaviour that indicates mental health support is needed.

Protracted grief

Sadly, anyone dealing with people who have severe disabilities, or mental or physical conditions that constantly deteriorate over time will know that their grief is ongoing. It is protracted. Day after day, sadness creeps in. It will sometimes be pushed aside, and other times may engulf you. Little by little, grief becomes a way of life. When the loss finally eventuates it is common for people who have lived in protracted grief situations to feel nothing. It is as if they are all grieved out. Clients have expressed feelings of guilt about not being in grief. Their grief has been so protracted that their energy is totally depleted.

11.3. On taking grief home

If you are working on a daily basis with people in dreadful situations, or who are engulfed by grief, it is important to be disciplined about not taking other peoples' problems home with you. I am often asked by clients how I can bear to do so much therapy/counselling work. In truth, there is the occasional day when I wonder if I can listen to another story of conflict or trauma, however, each client brings a story with such an honest yearning for change that my brain is attracted to the challenge of moving them to a place in their journey that is both personally rewarding for them, as well as socially responsible.

I learned early on that effective therapeutic work requires a strong faith in clients' abilities to choose their own life pathways. Following every counselling session the client starts a new journey that is hopefully different to the one they came in with. It is a journey I am not witness to until they return for a subsequent session. To dwell on or stay in the story that has just been presented means staying in the past. Once they have walked out the door they may be in a better or worse place, but they won't be in the same place. That moment in time has passed, and there is no point in staying there.

Once you tell your story, your journey changes. Taking responsibility for the lives of others is unavoidable if we are driving a bus, or flying a plane, or when someone is unable to take safe control of themselves. Any involvement in helping careers demands a cautious faith in the ability of others to choose their own pathway and a respect for their right to live their life the way they choose. 'Doing for' is disempowering for others unless they are incapacitated. Helping others to 'do for themselves' is empowering and satisfying for all concerned.

11.4. Life is about persistence and living with uncertainty

I have two close friends who had serious medical conditions that doctors had put down to depression or anxiety. Both were highly practical, creative human beings who made the most of every minute. Knowing these people well, I knew it was ridiculous to think that they would easily give up all their projects if there was not something really wrong physically. They may have been depressed, certainly; being unwell for a long period of time is enough to depress anyone. There had to be something else wrong, and there was! One recovered after emergency gall bladder removal, and the other recovered after emergency heart valve replacement.

You know yourself better than anyone. Trust yourself to persist when you know there is something wrong. Well-meaning doctors will diagnose depression when they do not have answers. Know and trust yourself. If you know you are depressed, seek help for depression. Be persistent when things are not right, especially with your health.

Whether it be a car accident, abuse, abandonment, or any multitude of things that shake your world, you have a choice to think like a victim, or like a survivor. Think about it; do you allow yourself to become constantly negative and cynical about the world you live in? The world can be a pretty confusing and frightening place. Does this kind of thinking render you powerless?

I know that some people choose to turn to religion because it gives them a sense of security. For some religion can become a way of escaping from uncertainties, taking on new faith in fundamental teachings. The ability to sit with uncertainty, means allowing yourself to see the grey areas behind issues that are often presented in a black and white, cut and dried way. Tolerating uncertainty is a healthy state of mind which requires the ability to tolerate a degree of discomfort and the ability to control anxious thoughts. It allows for the cautious development of a solid and reasoned stance before committing to a point of view. When there are no clear answers, you might be tempted to rush to black and white thinking. Calm yourself. There are many perspectives of any one situation. Do you really want to reduce your thinking to black and white answers? Is this how you choose to be?

Doing your own work
Talking to someone else about issues that are absorbing all your emotional energy is a sensible thing to do. It should not be scary or unpleasant, so refrain from constructing it that way in your own head. People go to therapy because they feel disconnected, either with themselves or with others. Everyone has a blind spot that they cannot see. Through talking in therapy about the things that are disturbing you, you have a unique opportunity to gain different perspectives from a person who is not part of your daily life. This person will focus on you, and you only. This person will not be judging you, but may give you perspectives that you have not yet considered.

When things go round and round in your head, it can seem like you are overthinking a situation. It is true that when you start to verbalise what has been silently thrashed out in your head it can start to feel a lot more real. There is a good and bad side to this. The experience of hearing the words as you speak them, and the experience of receiving validation and encouraging feedback can be liberating.

11. Grief, transition and change

Thrashing out the whole problem puts you in a position of being able to choose a course of action or thought, and clients report feeling much better than when they came into the therapy room. It is true that everyone has it in them to perceive what they need to do. Sometimes the necessary steps to achieve that are missing. Different perspectives light up new pathways. The tunnel vision that comes with anxious thinking is cast aside, and a broader perspective often results in a clear pathway.

Good therapists will not push you to talk about things you are not yet ready to talk about. They will not make you feel uncomfortable or ashamed, nor will they tell you what you should do. They are there to facilitate moving you to a healthier place.

Therapists practice different modalities. For instance, a gestalt therapist will help you identify your thoughts, your feelings, and your body reactions, and then help you reconstruct them in a way that will be better for you. A psychoanalyst works with unconscious processes. A family therapist looks at the ways families interact, join, and organise themselves. If you attend one therapist and you are not comfortable, look for another. Psychotherapists specialise in intrapersonal processes as well as interpersonal connection.

There are many different personalities in therapists, and many schools of therapy. Don't give up until you find one you feel comfortable with. It is a luxury to have someone's total focus, and sometimes the opportunity to express previously unexpressed feelings can take on true reality which will change your life in positive ways.

12

The wisdom of nurturing your soul

12.1. Believing in yourself
12.2. Spirituality
12.3. Going forward

12.1. Believing in yourself

The world is a crazy place, full of both wondrous and awful things. It is great to have a sense of justice, but at some stage we have to accept that life is not always fair. You can't win every argument, or force others over to the way you think. You can only influence others by giving them another perspective in the hope that they are open to receive it.

When you feel frustrated and blocked because others are stuck in what you consider to be ill-founded beliefs or ignorance, the best you can do is to search for the deeper point from which they diverge from yours. Search for the bit where they do agree with you. If they are closed off from hearing anything you say, save your energy and your action. Instead, look for convincing ways to be heard in more strategic circles.

When you find your passion, go for it. Don't listen to negative or pessimistic people. Believe in yourself and follow your passion. 10 years from now there's a good chance you won't even remember the names of most of the people you know now, so don't be dispirited by negative people. Aim for the future!

Know that while you might have many endearing characteristics, you are no different from other people when it comes to daily life, needs, and body functions. We are all ordinary human beings, though each of us have different hopes, dreams, passions, and strengths. That is what makes us unique. Everyone has fearful thoughts running through their heads. Everyone has self-doubt, hopes, and disappointments. What makes the difference is that some choose to dwell on those self-doubts, while others push them aside and forge ahead with hopeful thoughts. They choose to dedicate and persevere with what they believe in, and trust in themselves that they will get there if they work hard enough. They are passionate about what they want.

If you put other people either above or below you, you will find yourself in some circumstances feeling 'less than'. Your own judgement of others will return as you imagine others judging you. You don't need all that. Be inspired by someone else's efforts, but don't diminish your own. Listen to others, but value your own thoughts. Rather than worrying about what others think, celebrate your own efforts and how you feel about yourself for having given full effort.

Learn to go with the flow. Rather than stressing over exams or study tasks, put 100% focus into them. Work hard, over-prepare, then chill out. Enjoy each day. Remember, you will never have this day again. Do something each day that brings happiness to your soul. Take risks that will push you into new domains. Have a go! At the same time, be sensible and protect yourself from dangerous situations. Consider the risk. Avoid walking alone in dark places at night. Just don't do it! As a metaphor for life, if for some reason you have to walk alone, do it in a business-like way that indicates you have a purpose. Rather than saunter or muddle, walk confidently with your head held high, and be on the lookout for danger.

Think about who you choose to spend your time with and never be isolated for a long time with someone you really don't know. Trust without being foolish. Protect yourself physically. Try to build a life where your circumstances nurture your soul. Nurturing your soul is also about protecting your emotional self. Choose your friends carefully. How they conduct themselves impacts on your sense of self. The behaviour of your friends can easily become the norm for you. Be mindful of what it is that you are starting to accept as normal.

Some think of a soul as being the totality of ourselves; a combination of every aspect of ourselves, such as our thoughts, feelings, beliefs, and our awareness of our internal and external worlds. Whatever a soul is to you, know that when your head, heart, and body are all focused in the here and now, then you are in a good spiritual space and your soul is being nurtured. If you forget to nurture your soul by not experiencing the joy of being in the moment, you will end up feeling disconnected and out of sorts. You may even start listening more to anxious thoughts.

Take time to look to your internal awareness, to your hopes, dreams and yearnings. Observe what your brain has been processing and practise switching to your heartfelt emotion. Ground yourself by connecting with your senses and calm yourself as you move into the moment, the here and now. This is a pleasant state of being comfortable with both thoughts and emotions, both separate and together.

12.2. Spirituality

The ability to be in the here and now is a critical part of many spiritual practices and living mindfully. If you can achieve mindfulness in the here and now for a good part of the day, you will feel a sense of wellbeing. The sense of your own spirituality comes when you are fully-engaged and in the moment in something important to you, something you enjoy. When your head, heart, and body are in the here and now, you are in a good spiritual space. You might gain this from being within the family of your church, while sailing, walking in the forest or in your garden.

When you are in a good spiritual place, there often follows a sense that the whole of your world is greater than the sum of its parts, that you are more than the sum of your parts, that you hold something within you that is profound. Some find this in the exhilaration of sport, music, prayer, learning, or enjoying the environment. Remember, spirituality is not something that is owned by or only made available to you through a church or a religion. Find your own spiritual way of being in the world.

Be very wary of cults and groups that have a stifling religious or mystical belief system outside the mainstream religions. If you do join any type of group or following that suddenly engulfs your time or tries to control you in any way, regard this as a red flag. There are skillful persuaders who use narrowing processes to confine your experience of the outside world in order to bombard and seduce you – they brainwash people to become passionate believers by challenging your perceived lack of commitment. These kinds of groups usually seek financial gain and power, though their motivation might not be apparent at first.

When life feels confusing, these groups provide a highly social and highly tempting retreat from that position of living with uncertainty. They link mystical elements to their talk that are enticing. This kind of belief in mystical powers greater than yourself disempowers you in holding and shaping your own life. Promises of enlightenment and being lifted to a higher stage of awareness are often accompanied by cunning motivators. It is true that if you believe enough you can brainwash yourself into believing this greater being has changed your life. Be careful what you believe in! Trust in your own common sense.

Believe in yourself and your power to choose your own destiny, rather than have it allotted to you, or controlled by a suspect higher being. It is so easy to rush into subscribing to black and white views of the world that bring a sense of security because they seem to have all the answers. While it is much harder to live with the ambiguity, it is better than being sucked into simplistic and erroneous thinking which disempowers and uses you.

There are enough wondrous and mystical things in real life if you seek them. Think about what you want to change in your life, work towards that, and reap the benefits of satisfaction and joy in the lifestyle you have achieved for yourself. Enjoy the simple pleasures in life in the here and now. If mundane jobs take you down that path, then don't think they are beneath you. Rather than search for happiness or see it as a right, use your wisdom to know that it will come as a byproduct of dedication and commitment. It will come as a result of the way you choose to live your life. Following your passions will bring you to that magical sense of wonder and beauty. You have it within you!

Wisdom

Take time out to be with yourself. If you get too caught up in the world of others you can be swept into a world that is not yours. Monitor where your attention is. Do you wish to focus on supporting someone else, or do you need to focus on self-care, to appreciate silence and beauty? When you are stressed you miss the little things, the sparks of brilliance, and the joys of nature. If you take time to be in the present, to be more attentive in your observation of reality, you will regenerate your spirit and gain insight into your needs and wants. Wisdom brings you to appreciate your own spirituality in relation to others; it demands living with an unconditional openness to hold one or more views at once. Wisdom means living with an understanding that life has many shades of grey, and that nothing about life is simple.

Wisdom means having the ability to tolerate ambiguity and complexity, rather than holding on to rigid and simplistic views of the world because it is easier and less distressing. Rigid and closed thinking inevitably leads to judgement and prejudice. With wisdom you can learn to live with, rather than to fear complexity. Once you learn to do this, you are also able to appreciate the simplicity of life in the here and now.

Wisdom brings a sense of balance in changing contexts. No matter the situation, wisdom tells you that you will be okay. It means not changing yourself to suit the environment or social scene, but rather being yourself in every context. It means having a solid sense of yourself, regardless of the context. Be yourself, rather than what you think others want you to be! Believe in yourself and give space for your dreams. Know that determination and the power of the human spirit make anything possible.

Humility
Humility is different from wisdom, but is equally important. It is the idea of not having to win at all costs; not feeling better than, and not finding fault with everyone else. Humility is not always having to be right. It is realising that there is always something you can learn from another. To achieve humility, listen before you speak, and allow others to talk, rather than be dominated by your conversation.

Make room for others without losing the ability to stand up for something when it counts. Remember that people with big egos often have little, or no capacity to hear or learn from others. Humility recognises that our greatest gifts and greatest strengths in one context often prove to be our greatest weakness in other areas. Being a dominant and confident speaker in a debate may not equip us in intimate conversation. Similarly, being a kind and caring person who excels in putting others first may not be helpful in having your own needs met.

Humility brings the ability to adapt as you grow towards and through dreams that challenge you. It is an understanding that you have much to learn. You can habitually give up too easily when you fail, unless you have enough humility to own your failure, and to try again and grow past that failure. You can play games like 'poor me', or you can act in a belligerent way by refusing to have a go at things, or refusing to adopt a growth

12. The wisdom of nurturing your soul

mindset. This will work at first. It will get you out of things. Others will eventually back away and leave you alone. The trouble is, the end result will probably be that you feel lonely, have low self-esteem, lack personal dignity, and have your life experience narrowed. The worst part is that you will have done it to yourself.

It is so easy to stop yourself from growing or to block yourself from making the best of your life if you take too much notice of fear. The fear of losing face, of being embarrassed, of the unknown, of competition, of being shamed, that you will never change, or that you won't be able to handle emotional intimacy can be crippling. There are numerous fears that can block your development. Fear can block you at every step unless you learn to push anxious thoughts out of your focus. If you are open to new experiences you will understand that it is worth trying new things because you will always learn something. The more you learn, the more you will grow as a person.

If you want to be open to new experiences you need to draw on your strong emotional self to overcome every anxious thought that gets in the way of your wants and your dreams. Rather than hold yourself back, follow your heart. Push the fear aside and push through with what you want and how you want to be. If you add a little wisdom and humility you will have the perfect recipe for coming to appreciate who you really are. Your attitude to new experiences is what shapes your life. A positive attitude affects the way you learn and the way you take on challenges. Interest leads to connections with others and with new ideas. Out of dreadful situations can come positive experiences if you have the humility to connect with others, and the courage to engage in new challenges.

A positive attitude will propel you forward; a negative attitude will hold you static and unchanged. If you are negative, you will rarely see things in reality because you look through the lens of your own negativity. Think about what you do every day to invest in a positive attitude. You will find that when you take the time and trouble to look at things positively, everything around you will change. You can choose to change. You can choose what you want, and how you want to be.

Your attitude to success will reveal your arrogance or your humility. It is so important to take a little time out to feel good about what you have achieved. Arrogant people will gloat and broadcast how great they are. They will rub it in to those who have been defeated. Humble people will celebrate their success and feel for the person who 'lost'. A humble person will complement the defeated person on some aspect of their performance. They may allow themselves to be exuberant amongst family and friends, but they won't highlight the weakness of others, or make them feel bad or sad in any way. It is in your hands.

12.3. Going forward

Just as you connect in to social media, take time to connect in with yourself on a regular basis. When life gets too busy, you might notice that your thoughts are all over the place. The mundane things can seem more important than the essential things or you may be more in tune with what is happening in everyone else's life rather than your own. You might be irritable or resentful about the demands others put on you. If you recognise signs like these, make it your mission to take time out. Make doing nothing a high priority for a while as you gather your strength and your focus on what is really important to you.

Cherish good friendships and appreciate that the smallest gift of time is a treasure and may be all that another can give. Quality time is what sustains friendships. Be on the lookout for those who are judgemental, and those whose values don't include kindness to others. Stand your ground and be strong in the face of those who treat you poorly.

If your relationship falls apart, focus on what you have learned rather than what you have lost. Have the courage to

12. The wisdom of nurturing your soul

say goodbye to those who hurt you through some agenda of their own. If your family are emotionally supportive, respect and cherish them. If not, look around and identify the special people in your life who can regard as your emotional family.

If you come to a point in your life where you feel overwhelmed and unable to find something positive in your future, reach out to someone who can help you gain new perspectives. It helps if you are clear about the nature of the thoughts running through your head as distinct from what you are feeling. When your thoughts and feelings are all meshed together, it becomes very confusing. Make it a regular practice every day to ask yourself what you are thinking and what you are feeling in any one moment. As you express yourself, notice what difference it makes if you can distinguish what is a thought and what is a feeling. If you can't do it, work on it until you can. It might also help to check in with your body. Is it hungry, tired, holding stress, needing exercise? Are you in a good spiritual place? If not, then direct your energy to an activity that brings your head, heart, and body into the moment, working together. This moment is the only one that you need to deal with.

Remember, while your thoughts may be logical and rational, your feelings may be neither rational, logical, politically correct, appropriate, sensible, or justified. Nevertheless, your feelings are valid for you and they should never be discounted. When you become aware of your feelings, you will begin to identify what you want. Use the thinking part of your brain like a computer. Use it to help you work out the logistics of bringing about the change you want. When your head and your heart work together they form a powerful force capable of actioning any positive pathway you choose.

Every day brings change of one kind or another. Follow your passions, but be sure to ground them in gratitude for all you have now. Take time out to think about your dreams, but know that dreams on their own can be hollow. It is the journey that has to be enjoyed, so be prepared to modify your dreams as your situation calls for a change in direction. Be adaptable.

When you change who you are, it is like saying goodbye to an old friend – it hurts! You may feel uncomfortable for a while, but eventually the new you will look back at the old you as a thing of the past. There is always a silver lining if you are sufficiently open to look for it. Once you embark on any kind of change, enjoy the rewards that come with persistent hard work, dedicated focus, calculated risk-taking, and passion. Have fun all the way along your chosen journey!

Trust your own resilience and open yourself to loving rather than living in fear of being hurt. You will find someone who loves you for who you are, not merely for who they think you should be. When you find someone you not only love but like, respect, and trust, try to love them unconditionally. When you are open to loving selflessly, your own wellbeing feels less important than the wellbeing of the one you love. You will experience the full power of love that can bring both great pain and great joy. This is the kind of loving that occurs across generations, cultures, races, and religions. Some report this universal experience of love as the essence of their own spirituality. Regardless of whether this has meaning for you, when you open yourself to selfless love your inner world will be forever changed.

You can become whoever you want to be! Value your strengths, build on them and pursue your chosen pathway with whatever passion you have. You can change and build your personality and your character by consciously deciding the kind of person you wish to become.

Remember, life has its ups and downs, and without one there is no appreciation of the other. Without sadness, there is no full appreciation of joy. Even grief can bring an appreciation of life. Out of despair comes hope. Even less desirable emotions are evidence of you being alive and fully experiencing life. You can choose to play it safe by going through life like a robot, or you can choose to enjoy the exhilarating rollercoaster ride that life has on offer.

Work out what you want and choose how you want to be.

About the Author

Following an early career as a commerce teacher, Helen gained a Master's degree in Education Studies in 1993, and worked as a Guidance Officer in Queensland schools for 15 years. During this time she continued her studies with a two year post-graduate training program in family therapy. She became a Registered Psychologist and completed a second Master's degree in 2006 in Gestalt Therapy.

The same year, Helen moved to Hobart and worked in EAPs (Employee Assistance Programs) and in private practice. Missing work with young people, she took on regular days at *Headspace* in 2009, working with 12-26 year olds. She delights in working with adolescents who are often unguarded in the way they speak their mind, and open their hearts.

Helen gained generalist experience across a wide variety of contexts. In secondary schools she was involved in program development for tertiary entrance, pathways planning, student welfare, special needs, critical incident planning, and behaviour management. As a school counsellor she worked with students, parents, and staff. She also assisted students with career and academic counselling. Her employee assistance work involved trauma assist, manager assist and employee assist services. In private practice she continues to work with adolescents, young adults, couples, and families.

She looks back on her career having been honoured by the trust that young people, in particular, have placed in her. In her book she has highlighted the complexity of issues that confront young adults. She hopes the book propels them into wise choice-making throughout their lives.

Helen currently lives in beautiful Hobart, Tasmania. She is semi-retired, enjoys time with her grandchildren, travelling with her husband, keeping fit, and staying in touch with friends.

Notes

Notes

Notes

Notes

www.ingramcontent.com/pod-product-compliance
Lightning Source LLC
Chambersburg PA
CBHW021059080526
44587CB00010B/304